To:

_____

Date:

_____

When you forgive, you in no way change the past—

but you sure do change the future.

BERNARD MELTZER

Honor Books® is an imprint of
Cook Communications Ministries, Colorado Springs, Colorado 80918
Cook Communications, Paris, Ontario
Kingsway Communications Ltd., Eastbourne, England

The Gift of Letting Go—Powerful Stories of Forgiveness
© 2005 by BORDON BOOKS

Developed by Bordon Books
Manuscript compiled and edited by Betsy Williams of Williams Services, Inc.,
Tulsa, Oklahoma in conjunction with Bordon Books.
Designed by LJ Designs

ISBN: 1-56292-225-4

The
GIFT *of*
LETTING
GO

POWERFUL STORIES OF FORGIVENESS

COOK COMMUNICATIONS MINISTRIES
Colorado Springs, Colorado • Paris, Ontario
KINGSWAY COMMUNICATIONS LTD
Eastbourne, England

TABLE OF CONTENTS

Forgiveness unleashes joy. It brings peace.

It washes the slate clean.

It sets all the highest values of love in motion.

JOHN MACARTHUR

INTRODUCTION

Imagine an eagle taking flight. The air supports the eagle as it circles far above the earth, plunges into a steep dive, and swoops back up for another run. The eagle appears serene, even joyful, as it glides effortlessly through the air.

Now imagine what it would be like for an eagle if it were held captive. Assuming it receives adequate food and water, the bird could survive for many years. But could that eagle be content? Or would it always long for the freedom of the skies?

Perhaps you identify with the eagle. You long for freedom but are imprisoned by unforgiveness. Holding on to anger, bitterness, and resentment robs you of joy and takes the pleasure out of living. By refusing to forgive, you spiritually and emotionally bind yourself to the one who hurt you. You will never be free until you let go.

No one claims that forgiveness is easy. Forgiveness begins with a decision, and the journey is difficult. However, as you will read in the accounts that follow, those who forgive experience a light heart, energy, and joy. Once again, they are free.

As you approach each account, begin by asking the Holy Spirit to speak to you and to help you see the application in your own life. Open your heart as He prepares you to receive *The Gift of Letting Go*.

The most marvelous ingredient in

the forgiveness of God is that he also forgets,

the one thing a human being can never do.

Forgetting with God is a divine attribute;

God's forgiveness forgets.

OSWALD CHAMBERS

The Forgiveness of God

Forgive as the Lord forgave you.

Colossians 3:13

"Free at last! Free at last! Thank God Almighty, we're free at last!" No doubt you are familiar with this quotation taken from the famous speech by Dr. Martin Luther King Jr. Yes, the great civil-rights leader had a dream, but God the Father has a dream too—a dream that includes you!

But in order to fulfill that dream, you must first realize that there is no real freedom without a relationship with the God who provides freedom from the power of sin and death. Without spiritual freedom, all other liberties provide only temporary relief. But "if the Son makes you free, you shall be free indeed" (John 8:36 NKJV). The apostle Paul said it this way: "When someone becomes a Christian, he becomes a brand new person inside. He is not the same anymore. A new life has begun!" (2 Corinthians 5:17 TLB).

Paul wrote those words with authority because he had first-hand experience with the transforming power of God. Before encountering Jesus, Paul committed terrible atrocities against the believers. For example, the book of Acts says, "Paul was in complete agreement with the killing of Stephen" (Acts 8:1 TLB). More than that, "Paul was like a wild man, going everywhere to devastate the believers, even entering private homes and dragging out men and women alike and jailing them" (Acts 8:3 TLB).

But on the road to Damascus, everything in Paul's life changed. In an instant, Paul was dramatically transformed, and he became a brand-new person inside. The change was so striking that it caused him to serve Jesus Christ and never look back. As a result, Paul said, "I am focusing all my energies on this one thing: Forgetting the past and looking forward to what lies ahead" (Philippians 3:13 NLT). The only way Paul could fulfill his divine destiny and become one of the most influential figures in the entire history of the Church was through the freedom that God's forgiveness provided for him.

As Paul grew in understanding, he wrote: "Those who receive God's abundant provision of grace and of the gift of righteousness reign in life through the one man, Jesus Christ" (Romans 5:17). Paul's life is certainly proof of God's grace. God's forgiveness transformed Paul's life and prepared him for greatness in the kingdom of God.

Mary Magdalene was also changed by God's forgiveness. Held captive in a life of prostitution and sin, Mary's only hope was Jesus. And when Jesus forgave her, Mary left her old, sinful life to serve Him.

Are you bound by sin today? Do you feel separated from God—too guilty to face Him? Do you think that what you have done is so bad that there is no hope for forgiveness? If so, take heart. God has been with you since the day you were conceived. He knows everything about you.

Like the prodigal son in Luke 15, it's time for you to go the Father. Your Father sees you from afar and is running toward you with His arms open wide. Your Father wants to hold you close and set you free.

BIG MAC

by Mac Gober

Jesus Christ came into the world to save sinners.

I'm proof—Public Sinner Number One—of someone who could

never have made it apart from sheer mercy.

1 TIMOTHY 1:15-16 MSG

Vietnam! Humidity . . . sickening smells . . . death . . . lonely nights on patrol ducking enemy fire . . . screams ringing in my ears . . . my buddies cut down before my eyes. I prayed my own end would come quickly.

I went to Vietnam looking to become "somebody." There I vented the rage that had built up during my childhood—a wandering existence colored by alcohol and the absence of love. Daddy only taught me two things: how to shoot a pistol and how to fight. In Southeast Asia, I learned karate and went into the bush to train others in hand-to-hand combat. I felt important. But as soon as I returned—even with a pair of distinguished service medals and three decorations—my self-worth vanished. I didn't receive the recognition I had expected—certainly not that of a hero who had proudly served his country.

When America turned a cold shoulder, I turned to a group

of bikers who admired my military service. They seemed to be the only ones standing up for America's fighting men. Searching for a new status symbol, I bought a big red Harley Davidson. I hung out at bars and met a few riders, gradually becoming one of the boys.

But my new association did nothing to relieve the anger and resentment seething inside me. I covered it with a big attitude and a drug habit. I was trouble waiting to explode. If someone threatened me, I'd laugh.

"Big deal! I faced gunfire for a year, you think that scares me?"

I wore long scraggly hair and a huge bushy beard. A string of fights left me with no teeth, other than two fangs hanging down at the corners of my mouth. I was ugly, and I stunk. Though I acted brave, I was filled with fear. I landed in jail so many times that I soon lost count. Three marriages came and went.

I am not proud of living through hell for thirty years. I recount these events for only one reason—so others will understand that no one is too bad, too messed up, or too far gone to receive God's forgiveness.

God's grace first made an impression on me when I passed a little guy passing out leaflets. I took the piece of paper without thinking. When I tried to toss it to the ground, it stuck to my thumb. So I read it, and the message intrigued me. It said most people never make it to heaven; they think they have to get rid of all their bad habits, go to church, and be good before God will have anything to do with them.

"That's a lie," the leaflet said. "God commended His love toward you. While you were still a sinner, Christ died for you.

In the darkest hour of your life, Jesus got on that cross and died for you, regardless of what your sin might have been."

I was blown away. A couple of weeks later, I stopped at an apartment where drug addicts hung out. When I opened the door, I saw a pamphlet lying on the floor and picked it up. It was about God.

What is this? I thought. *Everywhere I turn it's God, God, God.* But I read it and started thinking, *What if God is real? If He is, I'm in trouble.* Just then, a pal staggered out of the back room.

"Where did you get this?" I asked, holding out the flyer.

"An old woman was passing them out. I punched her in the mouth and ran her off."

I will forever be grateful to that anonymous saint who had the guts to leave her four church walls and minister in a tough neighborhood. For two weeks I thought about her. What kind of love does she have that she would go out and knock on the doors of strangers?

She was still on my mind the night I returned to that apartment. Entering an upstairs room in the wee hours of the morning, I saw something that scared me more than any Vietnam firefight. I had a vision of Jesus hanging on a cross. Instantly I realized the truth—Christ had died for me. Not just for the world. For me—a smelly, dirty, rotten hoodlum who terrorized those around me. I burst into tears.

I love you, Mac, the Lord said.

That made me cry even harder. Shaking my head, I said, "But You couldn't love someone like me."

I could understand God loving good, honest people who worked hard and paid their bills. But the world's filth? I wasn't worth walking across the street to spit on. Nobody cared about me.

Mac, I love you, He repeated.

"You couldn't love me," I said. "Don't you remember all the things I've done?"

Mac, I love you, came the answer deep within my heart as I fell to my knees and cried.

Until Jesus filled my heart, I never knew such love existed. When I discovered it, I wanted to spend the rest of my days telling people the truth about Jesus. I made two requests that night. I asked Him to let me find my mother and apologize for all I had put her through. And I asked Him to let me help young people find the truth, so that they could avoid the mistakes I had made.

When I found Mom, she lay mired in alcoholism.

"Mom, can you ever forgive me?" I sobbed. (I used to fly into rages and drag her across the floor by her hair.) It wasn't until four years later, but she eventually gave her life to the Lord and spent eleven years serving God before she died.

I started attending a little church and quickly figured out that people weren't breaking down the doors to get inside. So I started going into bars and parties to reach them.

One night I talked to an old boy for two or three hours. Finally, I told him the truth: "You need to get saved."

"Okay," he replied.

Now what? I thought. But I quickly remembered that my pastor lived next door to the church. When we got there, I banged on the door. He greeted the two of us in his bathrobe.

"Mac, it's midnight," he pointed out.

"I know, but I've got a sinner, and he wants to get saved,"

I grinned.

Bless his heart. That pastor opened up the church and led that man to Jesus. After repeating this scene a couple of times, the pastor gave me my own set of church keys so I could go in anytime I wanted.

I began hauling in visitors by the carload. That little old church grew into a big one. Several months later, an elderly man came to me crying, "Ever since you started coming here with that big old crazy grin of yours and inviting people, every Sunday someone's getting saved," he said. "We're having baptisms every week. Families are coming together. Young people are coming in laughing. We haven't had that in forty years. We've all been saved, but we forgot to go out and tell others what Jesus did for us. I just want you to forgive us as a church for forgetting."

That was easy because I knew how much God had forgiven me. And I never forgot those bikers, drug addicts, and thieves who were my friends. Now God uses me in ministry to them full time.

Canaan Land Ministries has a one-year Bible training center for men. We help men get their GEDs, learn a trade, and get grounded in God's Word. We do this without charging a dime or depending on government funding. I've spent the last twenty years watching God pour out His grace and forgiveness on others, setting them free, and giving them new lives—just as He had done for a smelly old "Big Mac" so many years before.

THE MANSION BUILDER

by Dennis Jernigan

He Who began a good work in you will continue until the day of Jesus Christ . . . developing [that good work] and perfecting and bringing it to full completion in you.

PHILIPPIANS 1:6 AMP

When I was a child, my family lived on my grandparents' farm just outside the small town of Boynton, Oklahoma. From an early age, the Lord gifted me with the ability to play the piano; and by the time I was nine, I was regularly playing for the First Baptist Church. Although I mostly played by ear and had no formal training, my Grandmother Jernigan taught me to play chords for "church music." Also, she was the one who told me there was more to a relationship with Jesus than getting saved. I grew very close to this godly woman, but it would be many years before I would realize the full impact that she had on my life.

My relationship with my parents was typical for my generation. While I felt affection from my mother, I never remember receiving physical affection from my father or brothers. As I have grown older, God has reminded me of the many ways my father did express affection and love for me as I was growing up. My problem was not my father; it was that I believed a lie. And once Satan got his foot in the door of my heart, I perceived any rejection—no matter how big or how small—as a lack of love from my dad.

As far back as I can remember, I found it hard to believe anyone loved me. Consequently, my faulty beliefs prevented me from receiving love. And even though my daddy and mama never missed one single event that I was involved in—which should have spoken volumes about their love for me—I still chose to believe a lie. What I discovered, however, was that if I performed well, people would like me. Soon my outward performance began to hide the deepest hurts and failures within my heart.

I allowed rejection to permeate every part of my life, including my sexuality. Because I felt rejected by the most important man in my life, I responded by rejecting him and began yearning for intimacy with a man in perverse ways. Consequently, I came to believe I was homosexual. I remember having those feelings for the same gender at a very early age, although I hid this from others through my college years—with the exception of those with whom I had relations. Amazingly, in retrospect, I can see that the awesome and mighty hand of God was ministering His love to me even in the midst of my sin and confusion.

Because of my lack of formal musical training while growing up, my musical studies at Oklahoma Baptist University taught me a whole new language. Reading and writing the music that I could previously only hear and play opened up a new world for me. This knowledge would be very valuable later in my life as I began to express my heart and my feelings in song.

A major turning point for me came in 1981 when I attended a music concert by a group called The Second Chapter of Acts. I was looking for anybody who had an authentic walk with the Lord. I knew by their words and music that these people were genuine and that their message was born out of times of desperation in their own lives. As I listened to Annie Herring speak and sing, I was overwhelmed by the love she spoke of.

This was the love I had dreamed about, but I still couldn't believe this love was available to me! Then a phrase from the song "Mansion Builder" caught my attention: "Why should I worry? Why should I fret? 'Cause I've got a Mansion Builder who ain't through with me yet."[1]

Suddenly, she stopped in the middle of the song and said, "There are those of you here who are dealing with things that you have never told anyone else about. You're carrying those burdens, and that's wrong. You would be devastated if you thought anyone knew. You need to know that God sees and knows and loves you anyway. We are going to sing the song again, and I want you to lift your hands to the Lord. Place all of your burdens and hurts into His hands and let them go."

As I lifted my hands, God became more real to me than I had ever imagined! My hands became an extension of my heart. I realized that Jesus had lifted His hands for me—on the cross. I also realized that He was beside me and that He was willing to walk with me, carry me, and be honest with me. And I could be honest with Him! At that moment, I cried out to God and lifted those burdens to the Lord. I said, "Lord Jesus, I can't change myself or the mess I'm in—but You can!" And He did!

At that time, I acknowledged the fact that I was totally helpless and turned everything in my life over to Jesus—my thoughts, my emotions, my physical body—and my past. I took responsibility for my sins and yielded every right to Jesus—including my right to be loved and even my right to life.

Because of my sin, I deserved death and hell—but I began to hear the Lord speak to my heart. *Dennis, I love you. I have always loved you! You are My child, and I love you, no matter what, always!* It was then that I lost the need to be accepted or loved by others. I realized Jesus would love me and accept me, no matter what—even when I was rejected by others! It was at this time that my sexually perverse thoughts and desires were changed, and God began to replace them with holy and pure thoughts about the true meaning of sexual love.

Another turning point came in 1981 when a close friend found out about my past. I was certain that I would be disgraced and rejected. But this friend told me he loved me and was willing to stand with me as I walked through this time of deliverance. Then God began to bring others who were willing to love me and walk with me on my journey to complete healing. One of those people is my lovely wife, Melinda, whom I married in 1983. The Lord spoke to me when I was about nine years old and said that I would someday have a large family—with nine children! God has been good to us, and now we enjoy all nine of the children He promised!

In the 1980s, I hid my past, and only a handful of people were aware of my earlier failures. Consequently, my relationships were never truly be what God wanted them to be—because in true love there is no fear. I realized that God wanted to transform my worst failures into my greatest strengths.

Hiding my weaknesses deprived me of fellowship and kept me from loving Jesus freely. Furthermore, I realized that if I confessed my past, Satan would have less ammunition to use against me. So in July of 1988, I shared my past with my church. People came out of the woodwork—those who had been hurting just like me! And Jesus began to heal them.

Since then, God has called me to tell others what He has done for me and to lead others into intimacy with Jesus through music and worship. It was after such a time of sharing in my hometown that I began to realize the depth of God's love for me, the calling upon my life, and the role my grandmother had played. After the service, one of my grandma's former prayer partners came up to speak to me.

She said, "Isn't it wonderful how your grandmother's prayers have been answered?"

Surprised, I asked, "What prayers?"

"Didn't you know? Your grandmother told me that she used to stand behind you as you practiced the piano each day, asking God to use you mightily to lead in music and worship! And He has answered her prayers!"

As wonderful as that is—and I am so humbled and thankful—I realize that the Mansion Builder isn't through working in me. I can't make it through even one day without Him. He is the Father who will never leave me or forsake me, who enjoys my presence more than I could ever enjoy His! And as I continue to yield myself to Him, He will continue to change me every day to become more and more like Him.

HOMECOMING

by Lois Williams

You were like sheep going astray, but have now returned to the Shepherd and Overseer of your souls.

1 PETER 2:25 NKJV

For me, forgiveness is a story of loss and restoration. It is the story of a lifelong battle against bitterness and resentment sprinkled with little snippets of grace. God's grace kept me from completely abandoning my faith and gently pushed me toward the peace I craved.

My loss began with my mother's death from polio when I was nine years old. She was thirty-nine and had recently given birth to twin girls—making me the eldest of six children. In September of 1952, the polio epidemic was virulent, and there was no vaccine to prevent the spread of the disease. It took only a week for our lives to change forever. Daddy took us in his arms and told us he would have to be both mother and daddy to us from now on. That is how he broke the news to us that Mother was gone.

Being a preacher's daughter, I felt a huge responsibility to uphold and help him. At my mother's graveside, I remember wondering: *How should I react? If I cry, the church people will*

*think I don't know that she's gone to Heaven. If I don't cry,
they will think I don't understand that she is really gone.*

That began my life of appeasement—of people-pleasing,
pain-denying, phony living. Pleasing people became my defense
mechanism.

And the cycle of loss continued. Although it broke his
heart, my father gave my twin sisters to our aunt and uncle to
be raised. He vowed to get all of us back together; but sadly,
our family was never reunited. My aunt and uncle showered
the twins with affection and care, and our family remains close
today. However, the whole family suffered from the loss of the
intimacy that comes from living together and sharing experiences.

But I believe the separation was the hardest on Daddy. He
remarried with the hope of reuniting us. However, instead of
offering my father support and love, a large segment of his
congregation removed their membership and caused a break in
the church. Daddy took this failure to hold the congregation
together very personally. In addition, my maternal grandparents blamed him for our mother's death and were verbally cruel
to him. I lost my fun-loving father and learned to live with a
stern disciplinarian instead. Daddy kept a tight rein on all of us
so that there would never be another reason for anyone to
blame him.

As for me, I was angry at God—a terrible sin in my child-
ish mind. As a result, I took great pains to be perfect so that
God wouldn't have any excuse to cause me any more trouble.
Because I was a preacher's kid, the pressure to behave was
strong to begin with. The kids in my family were expected to
behave in such a way that no one could ever find fault with us.

Trying to please a Supreme Being with whom I was very angry was an effort in futility! I didn't acknowledge my anger, so it grew into bitterness. Later, I became a master at sneaky rebellion. I learned how to be very careful and not to get caught doing something wrong because I was afraid of the "church people's" finger-pointing.

Those words pretty accurately characterize my young adult and middle-aged years. Outwardly I appeared to have it all together, but inside I was like a quaking bowl of black Jell-O. And the blackness threatened to undo me. I never realized it was anger. I never even knew the source of the bitterness. I couldn't. And I hated myself because I saw the darkness that nobody else could see. I quivered with fear—terrified that the anger would come out one day.

Oh, how I needed forgiveness! And, oh, how I denied it. Voicing my need for forgiveness would reveal the sin, and I wasn't prepared to do that.

And yet, despite my anger and rebellion, God pursued me. He desired for me to know Him—not the God I had made my enemy, but the God who created me and longed for my love in return.

My spiritual illness was wreaking havoc with my physical health—including some serious neurological symptoms that the doctors investigated with a host of medical tests. During this time, my husband and I went to a Young Life's Malibu camp for a weekend—and I took my defiant heart along with me. In my cabin were five other women—young, beautiful, blonde, and slim. I was none of those things! As usual, I retreated into my shell of envy and discontent.

After cabin time one evening, a woman of God, to whom I

will forever be grateful, remarked, "I feel that we should pray for Lois." Earlier I had shared my physical problems with her. When the woman suggested that my physical problems might be related to a spiritual problem, I was insulted. I had worked hard to portray the image of a perfect Christian woman. But the speaker we had just heard had challenged us to really look inside ourselves, so I reluctantly agreed to have them pray for me.

Those lovely women gathered around my bunk, and their prayers began to lift me to the throne of God. I do not remember a word they said; I only remember the bitterness and anger that surged to the surface. I wept as I never had before. Gently they encouraged me to name the pain, acknowledge the loss, forgive my father, and forgive my mother for leaving me. And finally, with a wail of anguish, I asked God to forgive me. So many times I had walked the aisle because I felt the need to "get things right." I would pray a token prayer and feel better for a while, but it had never touched the real darkness inside of me.

That night, however, was different. I told God of my fury toward Him—how I had been filled with anger and resentment most of my life. Thoughts and feelings that I had never allowed to come out of hiding were opened to the light of God's love. As my new friends prayed me through the confessions, I began to sense a tender peace—a homecoming. At last I was able to receive the healing forgiveness that I had needed. I was free!

That night my life changed. My neurological symptoms slowly disappeared. I scarcely noticed the physical changes, however, because of the brand-new tenderness I felt inside as I experienced real joy for the first time in my life. I had finally come clean with God, and He had graciously cleansed my heart.

Sometime later, I walked into a bookstore and a painting caught my eye. It was entitled When I Come Home to Jesus, and it pictured a man crossing a bridge. In the painting, Jesus met the man in the middle of the bridge and put His arms around the man in a tight embrace. My tears erupted afresh at this visual reminder of what had happened between me and my heavenly Father the night He set me free.

When the struggle to accept God's forgiveness surfaces, I am reminded of God's promise: "I will sprinkle clean water on you, and you will be clean; I will cleanse you from all your impurities and from all your idols" (Ezekiel 36:25).

Confession . . . forgiveness . . . cleansing. How precious are God's promises! His promise to cleanse me reminds me of doing laundry as a child. I remember the hard work as I hung all those clothes on the line. But the memory also includes the lovely scent of clean white sheets, damp from the washing machine, stretched out on the clothesline to receive the warmth from the sun. What complete joy there is in God's forgiveness. Pure cleansing water, purchased with Christ's blood, sparkles like the morning dew on my freshly cleaned, white heart. May my life always be like the fragrant, damp sheets hung on the clothesline, freshly sprinkled with God's forgiveness, stretched out to receive the warmth and light of His Son.

THE QUESTION

Author Unknown

The LORD says, "I, even I, am he who blots out your transgressions, for my own sake, and remembers your sins no more."

ISAIAH 43:25

As a young man, a country priest of a Midwestern parish had committed what he considered to be a terrible sin. All of his life he had carried this burden and believed that God could not possibly forgive him for the terrible thing he had done. Then one day an elderly woman in his congregation told him that she sometimes had visions and during these visions she would have a conversation with God.

After a while, the priest got up the courage to go to this woman and ask her, "The next time you have a vision and talk with God, would you ask Him a question about me?"

"What would you like me to ask?" she responded.

"Ask Him what sin it was that your priest committed as a young man."

The woman, quite curious now, agreed.

Some weeks passed, and the priest went to see the woman to ask if she had seen a vision. She replied that she had.

"And did you talk with the Lord?"

"Yes," she said.

"And did you ask Him what sin it was that your priest committed when he was a young man?"

"Yes," she said, "I did."

"And what did the Lord say?"

The old woman looked deeply into the eyes of the priest and said, "The Lord told me He could not remember."

God not only forgives our sins, He forgets them. God remembers them no more.[2]

FREE TO LOVE ONE ANOTHER

by Ellen Bergh

Jesus said, "Forgive us our sins, just as we have forgiven those who have sinned against us."

MATTHEW 6:12 TLB

In 1980, after ten years of marriage, I got involved with someone else—the Lord.

The party lifestyle my husband and I shared had brought me to the brink of insanity and death. When God tossed out the lifeline, I grabbed it. And when I announced my conversion to my husband, Clarence, he shook his head. He was too shell-shocked to believe my news could make any difference, and he continued to fill out the insurance forms from my latest trip to the lock-down psych ward. But God made all the difference—my craving for escape into intoxication or death began to lift. I clung to God and avoided joining my husband in our old pas-times.

Suddenly, my husband, Mr. Party, found himself hitched to the Purity League. My recovery baffled him, and he resented my new sober companions. Focusing on all my husband's shortcomings, I prayed for God to change him.

Over the next year and a half, I launched an assault to convert my heathen husband. Deciding he was a captive audience in the bathroom, I left full-gospel magazines and tracts for him to read, and shared my spiritual insights until his eyes glazed over. I became a pain to live with. Why couldn't he just get with it? When we went out to dinner, I nobly sipped my coke and watched with distaste as he ordered a beer to prove he didn't have a drinking problem. We had less and less in common due to my newfound "spirituality" and his "vulgarity."

One morning, as I whined to the Lord, I sensed Him asking, *Do you love Me?*

The question brought me up short. "Of course I love You, Lord. You gave me a new life."

Would you do anything for Me?

"Yes, yes. What is it, Lord?"

Love your husband for Me. I loved you while you cursed Me. Will you do this for Me?

Feeling ashamed, I apologized and asked God to give me His eyes to see my husband. I'd fallen into such fault finding. I needed to visualize a flashing neon sign atop my husband's head reading, "God's Property—No Tampering." To our mutual surprise, I soon found things to praise Clarence for. And my faith grew as I obeyed the Lord.

A few months later, Clarence's mother was diagnosed with terminal cancer. Several times, he flew to Denver to sit at his mother's bedside. Clarence read the Bible to his mother, hoping to comfort her as she drifted in and out of consciousness. Just as the Lord took my mother-in-law home to heaven, God used my husband's faith—that was born out of hearing the Word—to bring Clarence to himself. In Denver, Clarence received the personal attention he needed from his loving heavenly Father.

In time, I saw that I had wanted my husband to become a Christian for selfish reasons. But God loved Clarence for his eternal destiny. I had been impatient for a quick fix, but God knew our marriage needed a complete remodeling. The Lord had to bulldoze our old attitudes so that He could help us begin to rebuild on His foundation.

God's forgiveness is an awesome thing. By receiving God's forgiveness, we are free to enjoy an amazing life full of adventure with Him. And when we extend God's forgiveness to one another, we find that marriage is a bit of heaven right here on earth.

BETRAYAL OF THE BRIDEGROOM

by Pamela Sonnenmoser

If we are unfaithful, he remains faithful,

for he cannot deny himself.

2 TIMOTHY 2:13 NLT

A cool breeze drifted across the churchyard, causing the hem of my white gown to flutter. The anticipation of what was about to happen made me giggle nervously as I waited with my parents. It was almost time to enter the sanctuary. It was the month of June of 1977, and it was the happiest day of my life.

I stood there facing the pastor as he charged me to be faithful. He asked me if I understood my commitment. I understood. I said that I would love Him always. I knew with all my heart that the covenant I made was forever. As we rose from the waters of baptism, I felt closer to Him than I thought possible.

I never meant to betray Him. In fact, it was very innocent at first. I knew that I should be faithful to the promise I had made, but there was so much out there that I had never experienced. Early in our relationship, it was easy to spend a lot of time with Him. As I got older and busier, however, my time just seemed to slip away from me. It wasn't that I didn't want to be with Him. So many other things just got in the way.

Ten years later, I had almost completely walked away. I still called on Him when I needed something; but for the most part, I had lost interest. It was amazing that He still loved me. In fact, there was never a time that He wasn't there when I called. It wasn't His fault that my heart had grown cold.

By 1990, we rarely spoke. I still knew He would be there, but I really didn't need Him. Every time I tried to talk to Him, something or someone got in the way. I had betrayed Him in every way, and I didn't see how He could forgive me. He never did anything to hurt me, yet I ignored His love and turned my back on my promise to love Him always.

In 1991, I met an incredible man. He was handsome and sweet. He drove a nice truck and had served in Operation Desert Storm. I fell in love very quickly, and soon I began to make a life with him. The day we married he told me that he didn't love me, but that didn't matter to me. I wanted to be with him, and I just knew that he would love me eventually.

I was right. Within four months of our marriage, he told me that he loved me more than anything and could never live without me. I knew I had finally found the love that I had been missing for so long.

My life was wonderful. I had all but forgotten my first love. My husband became my life, and I lived each day to please the man whom I thought would always love me. He never meant to betray me. In fact, it was very innocent at first. He knew that he should be faithful to the promise he made, but there was so much out there pulling him in different directions. Early in our relationship, it was easy to spend a lot of time together. But as we got busier, our time just seemed to slip away from us. It wasn't that he didn't want to be with me; so many other things just got in the way. Before long we had grown far apart, and he found comfort in alcohol and the arms of other women. It seemed that the only time he ever acted like he cared about me was when he needed something. Eventually we separated. The betrayal was too much to bear.

But the oddest thing happened during this most desperate time of my life. I hurt so much that I thought my world would end, yet I could hear my first love calling. He still loved me. I hadn't called on Him in years, yet He was still there for me.

God's Word states, "Nevertheless I have this against you, that you have left your first love" (Revelation 2:4 NKJV). The church at Ephesus hated the betrayal that they saw all around them. Yet, they had also betrayed the Bridegroom by leaving their first love, Jesus Christ.

The betrayal of my husband brought me to my knees in front of the One whom I had betrayed. Yet, there He was, waiting for me to run back to Him and to let Him love me. In His nail-scarred hands, He held unconditional forgiveness for my betrayal. He didn't tell me how much I had hurt Him, just how much He loved me.

As the Bridegroom stretched out His arms of forgiveness to me, He taught me how to forgive. As He extended His free gift of grace, He taught me how to offer that grace to others. He taught me about mercy by giving it to me when I didn't deserve it. He showed me how He had protected me even when I had been adulterous toward Him.

Six months after I left my husband, I returned home. I had to let my husband know that I loved him. I told him that I would never leave him and that I was no better than he. I, too, had failed to keep my commitment to the One I said I loved. I had to forgive him. I had to show him grace and mercy. There was no point in telling him how much he had hurt me. I had to tell him how much Jesus and I both loved him. I had to let the Bridegroom reign in my life and in my marriage.

Today, my husband is a man with a heart for the things of God. He understands mercy, and he can love me completely. Unconditional forgiveness led him to bow before the One who became his first love.

DEVIL AT MY HEELS:
THE STORY OF LOUIS ZAMPERINI

by Andrew Knox, *The 700 Club*

God rescued us from dead-end alleys and dark dungeons.

He's set us up in the kingdom of . . . the Son who got us

out of the pit we were in, got rid of the sins we were

doomed to keep repeating.

COLOSSIANS 1:13-14 MSG

Born in 1917, Louis Zamperini was one tough character growing up. He recalls, "Fortunately, those who cared about me had the foresight to convince me to channel my energy toward running track."

In 1934, Louis broke the world's interscholastic mile record. His time of 4:21 stood for two decades. Then, the "Torrance Tornado" qualified for a place on the American Olympic Team. Louis was off to Berlin, the capital of Nazi Germany. In the 5,000-meter Olympic final, Louis finished eighth, but ran the last quarter mile in just 56 seconds—so fast that Adolf Hitler insisted on meeting him. Louis went on to star at USC and ran the mile in 4 minutes, 8.3 seconds, an NCAA record that stood for fifteen years.

Louis served as a bombardier in the Army Air Corps out of

Ayuka field in Hawaii during World War II. The search-and-rescue-mission on May 27, 1943, should have been routine. Unfortunately, the only plane available was a green hornet that had been used for salvaging parts. Although the men were reluctant to take it, the plane had passed inspection, so they set out.

Then, eight hundred feet above the sea, the green hornet's two left engines cut out, and the plane and its crew crashed into the ocean, eight hundred miles south of Hawaii. Only the pilot, the tailgunner, and Louis survived. Clinging to a life raft, they floated in the middle of sixty-five million square miles of water. None of the search planes spotted them, and one week later, nature began taking its toll.

"The sun was our friend early in the morning when we were cold, and then it was brutal the rest of the day," Zamperini remembers. "They say there's no such thing as an atheist in a foxhole. Well, you can multiply that a few times on a raft. When a person reaches the end of his rope and there's nowhere else to turn, atheism isn't going to help. The person is going to turn and look up, and that's what we did. We prayed.

"Then we had to learn how to survive off the ocean. Although we partook of fish and an albatross, which we killed with our bare hands, there were other things we ate that are not part of our food chain, but we were starving."

While Louis drifted across the Pacific, President Roosevelt signed his death certificate. Then, after twenty-seven days at sea, the men spotted an aircraft—and machine-gun fire. It was the Japanese. After a thirty-minute assault, thinking the men were dead, the Japanese left. Miraculously, none of the men were hit with a single bullet. But six days later, their thirty-third day at sea, tailgunner McNamara died. Then finally one day, they saw land. Unfortunately, they were spotted by the Japanese. They had spent forty-seven days on the raft, drifting nearly two thousand miles before being rescued . . . by the enemy.

They were taken to the island of Wotje. Too weak to walk, the men had to crawl. Within forty-eight hours, they were transferred to "Execution Island." Guards delighted in telling Louis about the previous U.S. Marines who had visited the island, all of whom had been executed by decapitation, Sumarai style.

He recalls, "The worst part about being in the cell was that 75 to 80 of the Japanese lined up in front of my cell like they were going to a movie premier. Every one of them either swore at me, threw rocks, jabbed me with sticks, or spit on me.

"At sixty-five pounds, with constant diarrhea, I was starved. But instead of handing it to me, they would throw a rice ball onto the floor. I'd spend hours picking up every grain of rice mixed in with the dirt."

On three occasions, Louis was even injected as a guinea pig for experiments, but he made it off Execution Island alive. After forty-three days of captivity, he and Phillips were sent to a POW camp in Japan, where he met Matsuhiro Watanabe— "The Bird." Watanabe was so relentless in his torture that Louis has chosen not to speak about it.

Near the end of 1944, the Japanese took advantage of their famous prisoner's star power, but he refused to read the Japanese propaganda over the radio. Consequently, he was sent to be tortured by The Bird again.

Finally, in September 1945, Louis Zamperini was liberated.

"The war was over, and I was alive, but it was a whole new life," he recalls. "I married Cynthia Applewhite, and we had a little girl. But I was still suffering tortuous nightmares, waking up strangling The Bird. One night I even tried to strangle my wife in my sleep.

"I also indulged in drinking. The more I drank, the better I would sleep at night, so I was out every night drunk. My wife finally decided to divorce me, but before she could, someone talked her into going to hear Billy Graham. She came to Christ, and because of her conversion, she changed her mind about divorcing me! I reluctantly agreed to attend the next Billy Graham meeting.

"I knew I was a sinner, but I didn't like the idea of someone else reminding me of it. My whole life I had believed Christ was the Son of God, but it was not in my heart. Somehow I knew that if I would believe it in my heart, my life would be different. There was a tug-of-war going on inside me. I knew I didn't possess the Savior, yet I still didn't want to, either. As John 3:19 says, I was preferring my rotten life to the light.

"Then I started having flashbacks of the life raft and prison camp. I remembered the thousands of prayers where I said, 'God, spare my life, and I'll seek You and serve You.' Yet, when I came back home alive, I never even thought about it until then.

"That night, I gave my life to Jesus Christ. I knew I was through getting drunk. I also knew that I forgave all my guards, including The Bird. I think proof of that is that I had had nightmares every night about The Bird, even after the war. But since the night I made my decision for Christ in 1949, I haven't had a nightmare since!"

The young boy who grew up always wanting to get even came full circle in 1950, when he traveled back to Japan to forgive the prison guards who had tortured him. Although he couldn't meet with The Bird, he spoke with many of the former guards, some of whom even accepted Christ as their Savior! Then, in 1998, Louis again returned to Japan—to run with the Olympic torch before the Winter Games in Nagano.

"I believe with all of my heart that 'all things work together for good to them that love God, to them who are the called according to his purpose' (Romans 8:28 KJV)," says this man who found the strength to forgive his enemies when he found peace with God. Christ is the only way to God, and our eternal life starts now by faith in Jesus Christ. That is the strength we Christians live by, and through Him, nothing in life can defeat us.[3]

HEART AND SOUL

by Wayne Hubbard

with Sandy Williams Driver

Jesus said, "I have not come to call the righteous,

but sinners to repentance."

LUKE 5:32 RSV

I cut my baby teeth on a wooden pew in a small country church. Momma took us kids to the clapboard house of worship near our home in Rocky Hollow, Alabama, every time the preacher opened the doors.

She didn't always have enough money to buy new shoes at Easter or a warm coat at Christmas for me and my four siblings, but we didn't care. We wore our tattered Sunday-go-to-meetin' clothes with our heads held high.

I was a good kid growing up and rarely got into any trouble. Everything began to change, however, after my fifteenth birthday. That's the year I took the first step in my father's footprints.

My daddy never went to church with us, not even once. He looked for his religion in a whiskey bottle. I climbed into the front seat of a blue 1955 Buick with him on one of those restless evenings and took a sip of the local brew made just down the road. The fiery liquid burned a trail down my innocent throat, but I liked it. Over the next few years, I went out drinking with Daddy on Saturday nights and attended church with Momma on Sunday mornings.

Two months before my twentieth birthday, I received a letter from Uncle Sam. I stayed in the Army almost two years; never going to Vietnam, but peeling potatoes in Washington instead. When I arrived back home, I barely recognized the thin figure on the hospital bed. Daddy was dying; it was emphysema.

Momma prayed for him night and day; and finally, faced with the reality of death, Daddy got saved. As a teen, I had wanted desperately to be just like my father; but after he found Jesus, I ran in the opposite direction. I preferred the bottle over the Bible, and those twinges of guilt on my conscience didn't bother me at all. I knew better, but I took another swig to help me forget.

After Daddy's funeral, preachers from all over stopped by and tried to talk to me, but I ran them off. Losing my father only pushed me farther away from those Sunday-school lessons of my youth.

Sometime before Daddy died, I had gotten married. She wasn't anything like my devout mother, and that's just what I liked about her. We lived hard and didn't slow down even after the birth of our son.

Scotty was a beautiful little boy and the apple of my eye. But soon after his eighth birthday, he became ill and was hospitalized for tests. "Leukemia," the doctors said. Deep in my heart, a remembered prayer tried to surface and beg for his recovery, but the words couldn't fight their way past the alcohol on my breath.

After a long battle with the horrible disease, my only child grew too weary to keep on living. He gave up the fight when he was fifteen years old, and we buried him at the top of the hill in the cemetery, not far from his grandfather.

After Scotty's death, my self-destructive lifestyle went into overdrive. My marriage fell apart, and I couldn't have cared less when my wife packed her bags and left. My days were filled with working long shifts at a local steel mill and drowning my sorrows in cases of cold beer at night.

Two years later, I moved in with a woman from a neighboring town. Like me, Brenda had been raised in a Christian home, but had long ago pushed her religious background to the far corners of her mind. We enjoyed each other's company, and the next nine years flew by in a blur of hard drinking and fast living. On Sundays, we stayed home to watch Dale Earnhardt burn up the NASCAR speedways in his legendary number-3 car. The afternoon of March 15, 1998, was no different, and I cheered for my favorite driver with cans of Bud Lite while Brenda cooked our favorite meal of hamburger steaks.

She went to bed around 9:00 P.M., but I stayed in the living room watching television. Suddenly, a wave of pain streaked through my body. Thinking it was just indigestion, I decided to go ahead and turn in for the night. Halfway up the stairs, another lightning bolt threatened to rip me in half. There was a vise grip squeezing my heart, and the pressure was unlike anything I had ever felt. I couldn't breathe, and I grabbed my chest while stumbling on toward the top of the steps.

Minutes later, Brenda's teenage son found me there. They rushed me to the hospital; and through a haze of pain, I remember a doctor with a grave voice saying, "Mr. Hubbard, you've had a heart attack."

During the night, the pressure in my chest gradually began to subside, but the heaviness in my heart grew worse. I knew that I had almost died. I also knew that I wasn't right with God. Memories of preachers' sermons and my mother's prayers mingled with the drug-induced fog swirling around inside my head.

Due to a blocked artery, the doctor said I needed a stint for my heart. Before the surgery that Wednesday morning, one of my uncles, a preacher, walked boldly up to my bedside. Unlike everyone else, he didn't ask how I was feeling, but instead said, "How is it with your soul?"

I couldn't answer.

The surgery went well, and I was released two days later. Previously when life had hurled troubles my way, I had solved them with another drink. But even though I was nervous and scared when we arrived back home, I didn't reach for the beer waiting for me in the refrigerator. I reached for God's Word, instead. In the pages of the Bible, I searched for guidance and a new path.

I had always thought I could take care of myself, but I slowly began to realize that I couldn't handle everything alone. I needed His divine intervention. As the physical damage to my heart began to heal, so did the emotional scars. The chains wrapped around me were loosening.

One Friday a couple of weeks later, I went with Brenda to the supermarket. The elderly cashier was a familiar face, and we chatted with her while she rang up our purchases. After telling her about my harrowing experience, she looked at me and asked, "How is it with your soul?"

I still couldn't answer.

"Can I visit with you on Sunday?" she begged. I nodded my head while Brenda gave her directions to our apartment.

Two days later, I sat on the sofa while Nadine and her husband knelt down on their knees in front of me and started praying. Sweet peace like I had never felt before washed over me.

With a humble plea, I asked for forgiveness from the sins I had committed. God had been waiting patiently for my prayer, and He gloriously saved my soul. That day, on Palm Sunday, He released me from the life of bondage I had been living under for so many years. I was free at last.

The following Sunday, on Easter, Brenda and I sat side by side on a wooden church pew. There were no teething marks on that smooth bench, but I knew that I had just come home.

Over the next few months, the thirst for alcohol that had controlled my life since that first sip in my daddy's car was replaced by a thirst for the Holy Spirit. I studied the Bible every available moment and quenched my parched soul with His Word.

Brenda and I exchanged wedding vows; and with her holding my hand, I accepted God's calling to the ministry two years later. My life was suddenly full of purpose, and I wanted to help lead others toward His saving grace.

Standing behind a pulpit on Sunday mornings, I love to share my story of how the power of God's forgiveness changed my life and transformed me into a new man. I'm still learning and growing every day; but by His mercy, I am strong—in my heart and in my soul.

MY LIST

by Sharon Hinck

The Lord said, "My grace is sufficient for you,

for My strength is made perfect in weakness."

2 CORINTHIANS 12:9 NKJV

The fluorescent light over the kitchen sink glared onto my messy list. Jam smudged the corner, and a tea ring blurred some of the penciled entries. Doodles, scratch-outs, and addendums scrawled across the page. The paper looked as crumpled and defeated as I felt—a perfect summary of my day.

At sunrise I had begun with a crisp white page, boundless energy, and fierce determination.

Every day I was lured by the same elusive goal. I'd live a life of victorious Christian service—pure of motive, loving in attitude, and fantastically productive.

Each morning, I wrote reminders to myself in hopeful, chubby letters.

• Be a woman of God. Read Bible first thing. Pray. Memorize verses. Prepare stellar Sunday school lesson.

• Be a wonderful wife. Pray for Ted. Encourage him. Don't nag. Don't complain.

• Be a marvelous mom. Get Joel and Kaeti to discuss their teen angst. Play Legos with Josh. Read *Runaway Bunny* to Jenny. Be patient. Be consistent. No yelling.

More pragmatic goals continued down the page. Drop off library books. Make stew. Teach ballet class. Write newsletter. Clean hall closet. Take vitamins. Return phone calls. Floss.

I patted my list, took a sip of steaming English Breakfast tea, and reached for my Bible. Time to tackle the first item on my list. I was reading through the Bible in a year. Today's chapters were from Leviticus. I plodded through a few verses about eviscerating goats, begging God to bring His Word to life for me.

Before insight could strike, my two high schoolers straggled into the kitchen. I abandoned my reading. "Good morning. What do you have going on today?" My voice sounded too bright, but I was desperate to grab these few minutes of conversation with them. "Did you get your history essay finished? Are you staying late for play practice? Don't forget that Dad's working late tonight. You need some breakfast. At least grab a banana."

Joel and Kaeti squinted at me like hibernating bears prodded with sticks. Kaeti blinked and shook her head. Joel made a vague growling sound. A car horn beeped from the driveway, and they aimed for the door.

I blocked their way for quick hugs, which they barely tolerated—so much for my warm connection with my teens.

I watched them climb into their friend's car and pull away.

Lord, keep them safe. Protect them from temptation. Help them grow in their gifts. Guide their steps.

"Mommy, we're out of Cheerios." Jenny bumped against my legs and held up her plastic bowl like an orphan begging for gruel.

I closed the front door. "You can have toast, instead."

Her face wadded up like a gum wrapper. "Noooo! I want Cheerios."

A balsa-wood airplane skimmed past my nose, and Josh charged along behind. He barreled into his sister, and they ricocheted off a kitchen cabinet.

"Kids, settle down." My volume dialed up with my tension. Ted strolled into the kitchen, buttoning his collar. "Don't use the downstairs bathroom. The pipes are still leaking."

"But you said you were going to fix them last night."

He shrugged and grabbed his briefcase, waiting for a goodbye kiss. My lips brushed past his in a hurry, one eye on the kitchen clock. Jenny wasn't dressed yet, and the school bus would arrive in twenty minutes.

After Ted left, Josh unearthed a permission slip I was supposed to sign and remembered that he had forgotten to write a book report. Jenny disappeared into her room and came back wearing three clashing colors that don't exist in nature and pouted when I told her to change.

In scant minutes, a banshee had replaced my children's mom. "Look at this room! You haven't even made your bed. How many times do I have to tell you to keep your shoes by the front door? What do you mean you don't have any socks? I just bought you a dozen pair." The shrill, frustrated voice coming from my throat was not part of my plan for the day. But somehow I couldn't stop.

When the school bus lumbered to a stop outside, Josh and Jenny scampered out the door with obvious relief.

I flopped into the kitchen chair and took a second sip of tea, which by now was cold. No time to get back to my devotions. I had to hurry to the studio to teach my morning class.

The list beside my Bible lay abandoned. An hour into my day and I'd already floundered.

Oh, well. The day wasn't over yet.

Halfway to the studio, I realized I had never thrown the stew ingredients into the Crock-Pot. A package of meat was thawing on the kitchen counter, breeding E. coli while I fought rush-hour traffic. We'd have to have sandwiches for supper tonight.

At the studio, I slipped into my role as teacher. The morning whirled past like my adult ballet students practicing their turns. My spirits rose. My effort to live a virtuous life was getting back on track . . . until I relaxed in the dressing room after class. One of the women complained about her husband, and we all laughed and contributed a few snide comments about men. A rush of shame hit me immediately. The jokes felt disloyal and unfair. My husband deserved better.

Lord, help me guard my tongue.

After class, I hurried to the library and grumbled to myself when a Volvo nosed into the last good parking space in front of me.

Lord, give me a grateful heart.

At home, the phone rang and I saw a friend's name on caller I.D. and let the machine answer. I was tired and busy and didn't want to hear her litany of problems today.

Lord, where is my compassion?

Josh and Jenny tumbled through the doorway after school for a quick report on their day and then ran out to play at the park. I prodded myself to go with them. Chase a soccer ball around. Be an active mom. Instead, I flopped in front of the television and watched a game show.

One by one, all my good intentions had evaded me.

Now it was bedtime, and I picked up my stained, wrinkled list of goals from the kitchen table. Item by item, the entries accused me. My quiet time with God had never materialized after the first morning's interruption. I'd nagged Ted, lost my temper with the kids, and missed opportunities to share my faith.

I pictured Crayola-red letters spelling Failure across my life.

Lord, what do I do after a day like this?

Three choices wooed me. I could wallow in a mud bath of shame, deciding it wouldn't be worth getting up the next morning. Or I could convince myself that I wasn't as bad as some other folks. I could congratulate myself for the few things on my list that I did accomplish and ignore the stirring of my conscience.

I sank into the kitchen chair, flattened out the paper, and followed a third choice.

"Lord, I've fallen short. Again. I'm so sorry. And I don't have the power to change myself. Please forgive me. Change me."

The familiar rhythm of confession and absolution pulsed through me like the flow of blood out from the heart and back again. No matter how often I came to God confronted by my guilt, He forgave me. Gratitude, relief, and awe moved through me with a deep sigh. Forgiven. My impatience, my selfishness, my itemized record of failures—all erased by God's love. I tore up my list and threw the pieces into the garbage.

Out of habit, I grabbed a fresh sheet of paper and a pencil. My hand hovered as I pondered my agenda for the next day. I decided to try something new.

In hopeful, chubby letters, I wrote one entry on my list.

"Live in grace."

Forgiveness is all-powerful.

Forgiveness heals all ills.

CATHERINE PONDER

THE POWER OF FORGIVENESS

Jesus said, "I tell you the truth, whatever you bind on earth

will be bound in heaven, and whatever you loose on earth

will be loosed in heaven."

MATTHEW 18:18

The domino effect. You've seen it. Someone painstakingly sets dominos on end and lines them up equidistance apart. Then the fun begins. With the slightest effort, the first domino is pushed over and falls onto the next, which falls onto the next, and so on until every domino has fallen.

What does that have to do with forgiveness? Quite a bit. To forgive or not to forgive is our choice—but both have a far-reaching effect. In fact, much more is set into motion than meets the eye.

Although you might not think so at first glance, when Jesus said, "whatever you bind on earth will be bound in heaven, and whatever you loose on earth will be loosed in heaven" (Matthew 18:18), He was talking about forgiveness. Could it be that when we refuse to forgive, we actually bind people in their sin and tie God's hands? On a personal level, we know that unforgiveness binds us in many ways. But this passage indicates that far more than personal bondage transpires. When we "free" those who have wronged us by forgiving them—letting them go—we not only set them free, but we also loosen the grip of pain around our own hearts so that healing can begin.

This is not to say that when others hurt us there should be no consequence to them. For instance, if the action of the perpetrator breaks the law, the legal system deals with them. Though forgiven, that person may still have to walk out the legal consequences.

In learning about forgiveness, it is important to understand what forgiveness is not. Forgiving another person does not mean that you condone their sin or deny its existence. It doesn't mean that you have not suffered as a result of their actions or that what has happened to you is unimportant. It does not mean that you should deny or ignore your pain. Sadly, it does not guarantee that there will be reconciliation.

What it does mean is that you have stepped down from the judgment seat. Instead of revenge, you let go of the offender and place them in God's hands. Instead of praying that God would judge the person, you pray for God to bring the individual to himself and for God to correct and heal the part of that person that is responsible for hurting you. Forgiveness means that you are not going to allow the experiences of your past to dominate your future. You are not going to allow the actions of others to keep you from fulfilling your divine destiny.

Just as negativity sets off a chain reaction, so does forgiveness. Forgiveness stops negativity in its tracks and begins a new chain reaction. The Bible puts it this way: "If he plants the good things of the Spirit, he will reap the everlasting life that the Holy Spirit gives him. And let us not get tired of doing what is right, for after a while we will reap a harvest of blessing if we don't get discouraged and give up" (Galatians 6:8-9 TLB). This means that when we plant the good seeds of forgiveness in the lives of those who have hurt us, then God is able to intervene and transform the people and the circumstances that seem beyond reach.

No doubt, forgiving those who have hurt us is one of the hardest things for humans to do. But as you will read in the pages that follow, when we take the first step and push over the "domino" of pain by letting go, forgiveness will not only transform us, but it will also trigger miracles in the lives of others.

The Candy Man

by Golda Browne

If any man be in Christ, he is a new creature: old things are

passed away; behold, all things are become new.

2 Corinthians 5:17 kjv

It was a blustery winter day. Dark clouds moved across the sky. It was just two weeks until Christmas, but this day was void of holiday cheer. Droves of mourners silently filed into the sanctuary. Except for the organ music, a somber hush permeated the auditorium. Already many were wiping away tears.

"Where's the candy man, Momma? Why are people crying?" little five-year-old Ginny whispered.

"The candy man's in Heaven. People are crying because they're going to miss him," her mother explained.

I hadn't expected to see such a young child at an elderly man's funeral. Then I noticed many families with young children who had come to say good-bye to the candy man—many not even knowing his name—but I knew him as Daddy.

The choir began singing, "Victory in Jesus . . ." As the music faded into the background, emotions engulfed me—my mind drifting back to when I was Ginny's age and my daddy was anything but the candy man.

I shuddered, remembering a morning long ago that exploded into a hellish nightmare of abuse.

"Didn't I tell you to make your bed?" my dad yelled, enraged beyond imagination.

"But Daddy, Uncle Charley's teaching me to tie my shoes. Look what I can do!"

Yanking his belt from his trousers, Daddy grabbed my arm; dangling me in the air, he started beating me unmercifully. Then trudging down the hall, he threw me onto my bed shouting: "You'll mind me, young lady, or you'll wish the h--- you had!" Out of control, this six-foot four-inch, 225-pound man continued flogging me.

Back in the fifties, Social Services didn't intervene. Several times, the beatings resulted in injury. I remember my mother taking me away to stay with relatives. I never wanted to go back home; but inevitably, Mother would come, and I'd find myself back in the nightmare. The trauma and shame left a very scared girl who grew up learning to hate as the abuse continued into adulthood.

Fortunately, in my twenties, I met Janice Wise—the kindest woman I'd ever met. God had moved her into my part of the world from Plumtree, North Carolina. Janice shared with me the gentleness of Christ's love and led me to accept Him as my Savior, which changed my life forever. Within weeks, the reality of the hatred toward my dad gnawed at my insides. I certainly felt entitled to hate this man—but in my heart, I knew the hatred had to go. The trouble was—how do you get rid of a lifetime of hatred that possesses your whole being?

"O God, I want to forgive him; I want to let this hatred go," I prayed every day. But no matter how hard I tried, it was just part of who I was.

Then one day while I was praying, God spoke to my heart, *Which is worse—your dad's abuse or your hatred?*

"But God, I've every right! Look what he's done to me!"

Then I heard the still small voice again, *Do you want to be free from the cancer of hatred or remain its prisoner?*

With tears rolling down my face, I knew I wanted to be free more than anything else. "Okay, God! Tell me what to do, and I'll do it—anything!"

"Anything" translated into God prompting me to go to my father and ask him to forgive me for hating him all my life— obviously the most absurd idea I'd ever heard of. I've learned since, though, that God's thoughts are much higher than mine.

It took me months to get up the nerve to face this giant of a man. Even as an adult, I still greatly feared him. During that time, God taught me a valuable lesson—He doesn't grade sin on the curve. Sin is sin! If my dad's part was 99 percent and mine only 1 percent, then my job was to take care of my 1 percent.

One evening, I knew it was time. With trepidation, I went to carry out my mission. When I arrived, the house was in shambles. The furniture was turned upside down; the den ceiling light dangled from its wires; lamps were broken; and items of sentimental value were aflame in the fireplace.

I walked trembling toward my parents' bedroom. Slowly nudging the door open, I found my dad sitting on the side of his bed. From the doorway, I delivered my well-rehearsed statement with a question attached (my plan being to then cut and run).

"Daddy, God has convicted me that I've hated you all of my life, and I know it's wrong. Will you please forgive me?"

"Well, that's just what kids do. You hate me. I hated my dad, and he hated his. That's just life! Now get out of here, and let me go to bed," he growled.

Once again, I came back with my preplanned reply, anticipating that he'd avoid my question. "Daddy, we both know that I've hated you. But hate has no place in God's plan. I need to know. Daddy, will you please forgive me?"

At that my dad lunged toward me. I flinched, stumbling backward. He grabbed my hand and pulled me down on the bed next to him. We just sat there for a moment, saying nothing—my heart about to pound right out of my body. Then I saw a tear roll down my father's face. Then another . . . and another. It was the only time in my whole life I had ever seen him cry. Then he looked at me and said, "Sugar, I've been one sorry son-of-a---- dad. I suppose I could forgive you if you could find it in your heart to forgive me."

It was the one response I had not expected—and the one that changed us both forever. My dad was never abusive to me again!

Over the next year, Daddy watched as the resurrected life of Jesus grew in me.

"Sugar, what's different about you?" he would ask.

"It's just Jesus!" I'd always tell him.

And then he'd say, "Don't give me that religious talk. Are you taking one of those positive-thinking courses?"

Sometimes it made me want to giggle. "No, Daddy!" I'd

say. "It's the love of Jesus."

About eighteen months later, Daddy agreed to go with me to hear David Wilkerson speak. At the close of the meeting, Wilkerson gave an invitation; and to my great joy and astonishment, Daddy was the first to stand up! He was fifty-nine years old; and from that day on, he was a visibly transformed man. Just a short time later, I was in awe when he invited me to come to his baptism—the proudest day I had ever spent with my daddy.

He started coming to church with me—Sunday mornings, then Sunday nights. After a while, Daddy was at church every time the doors opened. One day, he showed up at church with a sign painted on the back of his red jeep: "Follow me to Birchman Baptist Church—you'll never be the same." He only lived five more years—but they were the best of his life.

One of his favorite things to do became his self-appointed ministry as the candy man. He'd stop at the local grocer every Sunday morning and buy a huge bag of Brach's candy. Then after the worship service, he'd stand on the church steps and give candy to all the kids. This ritual endeared him to many children and families alike.

"Hey, Mom!" my daughter whispered, nudging me. "You look like you're in another world."

Tears rolling down my face as my dad's favorite hymn came to a close, I took the tissue she pushed into my hand.

"Victory in Jesus"—such a powerful hymn! I wiped my tears, struggling to clear the lump in my throat. Just as the lyrics affirmed, Jesus did come and heal my broken spirit—and my dad's, too! No wonder so many kids were present on that solemn day. In my dad's own simple way, God's love had flowed through him to each and every one of them! They had come to say farewell to the candy man. All I could do was thank God for that unsuspecting day when I received His grace to take care of my 1 percent.

THE TRANSFORMING POWER OF FORGIVENESS

by Charlie Osburn

Jesus said, "Love your enemies,

do good to those who hate you, bless those who curse you,

pray for those who mistreat you."

LUKE 6:27-28

"Daddy, I want to show you the fun we've been having." My eight-year-old daughter smiled as she dropped the magazine in my lap. "We've done some of the things they show in here."

Within a few seconds, my skin crawled. My little girl had handed me the filthiest pornography I had ever seen. It was so perverted you couldn't even buy it at the newsstands where they routinely stocked that kind of trash.

My next-door neighbor was a child molester. As the ugly story unfolded, I discovered that not only had he raped and molested my daughter for two years, but he had also victimized my son.

Since my wife had been busy running our restaurant, we had arranged for our neighbor and his wife to watch our two youngest children after school. We had every reason to trust him. We had known him for years, and his children had grown up with my wife.

He was arrested and tried; but because he was sixty-five years old, the jury recommended leniency. The judge gave him a ten-year suspended sentence, placed him on probation, and sent him home.

I seethed, "God, how I hate him!" on the day the last board went up on the eight-foot-high fence I erected to block my view of his house. I could feel my children growing resentful of my overbearing and suspicious attitude. I would never let such a thing happen again.

My unresolved hatred grew, and soon I was drinking in a futile attempt to soothe the rage inside. I wanted to kill my neighbor and fantasized about bombing his car, hiring a hit man, or tossing a torch on his house late at night. The fear of the legal consequences was the only thing that stopped me.

My obsessive hatred began to ruin my marriage. Finally, my wife and I separated. I left the restaurant with her and pursued my goal to work in real estate. That might have happened had I not failed the real-estate exam. I was back in town studying to retake the test when I ran into Father James Smith, a priest I had met when I joined the Catholic Church. Assigned to another parish, he had been away for fourteen years.

"Well, praise the Lord, Charles," he grinned when I greeted him at our restaurant.

When he asked how I was, I spent two hours moaning about my problems. He listened patiently and then replied, "Charlie, I've got good news for you."

Father Smith told me that Jesus loved me totally, completely, and unconditionally, in spite of myself. For a month I went to the rectory each week to see him. We talked for hours at a time.

"Charlie, you've got to give it all to Jesus!" he proclaimed every time I walked into his office.

Finally one day I shouted back, "Tell me what to give Him, and I will!"

Father Smith prayed with me that day; and as I surrendered my life to God, my heart was changed—but I still struggled with my feelings about the man who had harmed my children. Father Smith showed me Matthew 6:14-15 and Luke 6:27-35, the passages where Jesus talks about forgiving and loving our enemies. I couldn't believe what I was hearing.

"You mean, I have to love the man who molested my children?" I asked. "Why, he's a horrible human being! Even the thought of loving him makes me ill."

Finally Father Smith asked me a strange question. Which, he wondered, was worse—rape or murder?

"Murder, of course," I answered.

He then flipped to 1 John 3:15, which equates hatred with murder.

I brooded over his words for three weeks. Then one day, quite by accident, I saw my neighbor. As I backed my car out of my driveway, he was pulling into his. I hesitated for a moment then yanked the key out of the ignition and ran after him. When I approached him in his driveway, he threw his arms up in front of his face and pleaded, "Don't hit me!"

"I'm not going to hit you," I said. Then I forced the words out. "I've come to ask your forgiveness for hating you."

As soon as the words were out of my mouth, I felt lightheaded. My inner emptiness vanished, and the pain that throbbed in my chest was gone, too. How good it felt!

Leaving my neighbor with a slightly stunned look on his

face, I ran home and asked my children for their forgiveness, because my overreaction and the resulting family tension had caused as much damage to them as the molestation had.

My apology healed my relationship with my youngest daughter, but it took awhile for my son to reconcile. When he finally accepted Jesus six years later, he said, "Thanks, Dad, for loving me into the kingdom!"

With this festering spirit of hatred and unforgiveness abolished, I was ready to receive everything God had for me. A few weeks later, I was driving down the highway, and I was startled by the revelation that Jesus was now the Lord of my life—all of it!

I pulled off the road, lay down on the seat, and raised my hands toward heaven. When my own vocabulary was exhausted, I began to praise and worship God in the Spirit.

That simple act of obedience—forgiving the man that I had wanted to kill—unlocked a door to a personal relationship with God that was so wonderful, so powerful, so joyful that I've been shouting ever since!

Then another dramatic incident occurred. Three months after I forgave the man and asked him to forgive me, my wife saw him in the supermarket. He beamed as he showed my wife his New Testament and told her how he had given his life to Jesus. Three weeks later, my neighbor died. But in God's perfect timing, forgiveness had done its transforming work and had given him entrance into Heaven.[4]

Falsely Accused

by Anne Allen

I will sing of Your power; Yes, I will sing aloud

of Your mercy in the morning; For You have been my defense

and refuge in the day of my trouble.

Psalm 59:16 NKJV

I sat across from my husband, not believing the turn our lives had just taken. Brad and I loved the ministry. We enjoyed people and had worked hard as associate pastors. Our large church had many needs, and we were just getting started.

The senior pastor and his wife were significant to Brad and me even before we married. During my college years, our pastor's wife mentored me. And our pastor recruited Brad to serve as the singles' pastor in our church. Brad's energy and zeal for people caught the pastor's eye, and Brad's journey into the ministry began.

A few years later, Pastor married us in a wonderful ceremony, and we pledged our lives to each other. That day, we made a commitment to serve God and love people.

Later, as we rehearsed the accusations against us, that happy day seemed so long ago. Brad's supervisor at the church accused him of losing $90,000 of ministry finances during the previous year. Why would he try to sabotage Brad's job? Why would he accuse Brad of something he hadn't done? We couldn't understand what was going on.

Once the word spread, many staff members at the church offered their condolences. Others stayed away, unsure whether the allegations were true or not. We wanted to defend ourselves, but we had to trust God that the charges would be proven false in time.

The pastor's policy was for staff members to deal with their immediate supervisors to work out all conflicts. With a church the size of ours, the senior pastor could not be involved in every management issue. We understood that; but we felt close to the pastor and his wife. We naturally wanted to explain ourselves to them and receive their approval. Unfortunately, we now had a big question mark over our heads— even in the eyes of our pastor.

The months it took to work out the accounting problem seemed like an eternity. My husband's secretary did the record keeping, and the CFO of the ministry would examine her records. Even so, we were confident that the accusations were untrue.

Meanwhile, the black cloud continued to hang over us. We felt like Joseph—imprisoned for a crime that we hadn't committed. When we questioned our accuser in private, he admitted that Brad's termination was his motivation.

From the very beginning, Brad and I knew we needed to keep our hearts right. Many days it seemed impossible, but we worked hard at it. My thoughts would be so heavy from the weight of the lies that I had to repeat, "I forgive him, I forgive him, I forgive him." I didn't want to say those words. And I

didn't want to forgive. I wanted to shout that we were innocent! But we knew that God sometimes uses difficult situations
to build spiritual muscles. Our hearts had to be free from
unforgiveness.

For six months, the accountant worked on the figures.
Many times we wanted to resign our ministry position. Then
we could have gone to another church where no one knew us.
But we were locked in. To run would be defeat. Besides, running would only give temporary relief. God desired to deliver
us not just from the accusations, but from the right to defend
ourselves. He was to be our defense.

On and on we continued, "We are forgivers, we are forgivers, we are forgivers." Sometimes I believed it, but often I
was just saying what I wanted to be.

We were overjoyed when the CFO showed that we had not
lost the money. In fact, Brad's area of the ministry had been
able to pay for itself completely! We rejoiced and were grateful
that our troubles were over.

But the next week at the church, we sensed that our pastor
and his wife had lost confidence in us. They trusted our supervisor and did not see the inconsistencies in his behavior. Within
weeks, we knew that our time was up. We cried as we prepared
to leave the church staff. Our names had been cleared, but our
reputations had suffered a loss. As we sought the Lord, we felt
His direction was to step down quietly, giving no place for bitterness to take root.

After the first weeks of our resignation, Brad and I began
to talk about where we would like to go to church. We weren't
on staff anymore. We could go to any church. At least we

deserved a change of scenery, considering all we had been through. Yet, the Lord spoke very clearly to us and said, *Stay where you are. This is where you were hurt; this is where you'll be healed.*

We could not imagine why God would ask us to stay in a church where we had been so badly hurt. We understood that He wanted to deal with us and heal us, but why couldn't He do it somewhere else? Still, our direction was clear. God wanted us to stay put.

So we stuck it out—Sunday after painful Sunday. We were used to sitting on the front row, but now we sat in the back. We had been in the inner circle, but now we felt like outsiders.

Then, six months after we resigned our position, our senior pastor and his wife asked us to come in and talk with them. They apologized for not being aware of all that we had been through. Our previous supervisor's inconsistencies had been exposed. He was asked to step down so that he could get some help.

I believe that those months were a test. Not to see if we were tough enough, but for something far greater. When we were falsely accused, would we take on the same spirit as the accuser? Or would we be people who desired the Spirit of Christ? When Jesus was wrongly accused, He forgave. The forgiving Spirit of Jesus always wins over false accusations. He sees to it.

FORGIVENESS AS A WAY OF LIFE

by Rolf Garborg

Don't repay evil for evil. Don't retaliate when people

say unkind things about you. Instead, pay them back with a

blessing. That is what God wants you to do,

and he will bless you for it.

1 PETER 3:9 NLT

Everybody loved my father—everybody, that is, except Mr. and Mrs. Aune. They were neighbors on the lake where we lived for thirteen years. It wasn't a personal thing. At least it didn't start out that way.

Twenty years before we moved into the house next to theirs, the Aunes had a severe crossing of wills with a member of their church. Rather than resolve that conflict, they became extremely bitter—not just toward that other member or even the entire membership of their church. No, they were bitter toward anyone who attended church anywhere. And they told anyone who would listen.

The Aunes were in their midsixties when we met. When they learned that we were Christians, they wanted nothing to do with our faith or us. We tried to honor their wishes. But

God had other plans.

Our home was on a lake on several acres of land, giving our dog, Shultz, ample room to run. But somehow it was never enough, so he often visited the Aunes' yard as well. Shultz's trespassing especially bothered Mrs. Aune. She showed her frustration by shouting various things at him, none of which he understood. She even notified the town constable about Shultz. We tried to keep Shultz home, but when a boat pulling a water skier came close to our shoreline, a ball and chain could not have held him.

The day finally came when Mrs. Aune and Shultz had a showdown. She was out in her yard digging dandelions, using a picker with a five-foot wooden handle on one end and a sharp, twin-pointed blade on the other. When Shultz came flying through her yard, she wound up like a baseball pitcher and let the lethal weapon fly. Fortunately for Shultz, she was out of practice, and the lance sailed harmlessly over his back.

Within minutes, Mrs. Aune was pounding on our door. Having observed the encounter from the window, my dad offered to greet our visitor.

I'll never forget what happened in the next few moments. As my dad opened the door, there was Mrs. Aune, literally bouncing up and down with rage, like some plastic wind-up toy.

For what seemed like an eternity, Mrs. Aune screamed at my dad at the top of her lungs. When she could think of nothing else to say, she stood there sputtering like an old motor. Finally, she ran out of gas and stopped.

We listened as my father replied, "Dear Mrs. Aune, I am so sorry that we have upset you so. Will you ever forgive us? We'll try not to let it happen again. God bless you, Mrs. Aune."

For a brief moment, she stood there in stunned silence. She was defenseless. Then she spun on her heels and charged back across the yard.

For several weeks, we didn't see Mr. and Mrs. Aune, and Dad became concerned. Their lawn, usually nicely kept, was overgrown and in desperate need of mowing. So after considerable prodding from Dad, my brother and I were finally convinced to mow their lawn. We were about fourteen and sixteen years old at the time, and this wasn't how we had planned to spend a warm summer day at the lake. It was an all-day job to mow and rake their large lawn. But we did it, however reluctantly.

No sign of life appeared in the Aune house while we worked, but we knew they were home. Two weeks later, my brother and I protested as Dad asked us to mow their lawn again. This time we saw Mrs. Aune peeking from behind the curtains.

Two more weeks had passed when Dad looked over at the Aunes' lawn and said, "Well, boys?" We knew what that meant.

This time, just as we were finishing, Mrs. Aune came outside carrying a tray with a large glass of lemonade for each of us. She thanked us for mowing her lawn and explained that her husband, Al, had not been well. We told her we were sorry and were glad to help in any way we could.

Later that fall, Mrs. Aune called. "Can you come quickly? Al is very ill."

Mom and Dad rushed to their home. Mrs. Aune took them

to the bedroom where her husband lay. They talked with Mr. Aune about his illness, his past with the church, the state of his soul, and the redeeming blood of Christ that could make him clean again. Mr. Aune listened, thanked them, and asked them to please come back.

Dad and Mom visited the Aunes many more times after that. Finally, the day came when both Mr. and Mrs. Aune prayed to receive Christ as their Savior. I can still remember my parents' joy when they told us the story.

A short time later, Mr. Aune went to be with the Lord. Mrs. Aune joined our church, soaking up everything she could. The following summer she was baptized in Lake Wissota. She grew in her faith and became a close friend of our family. Then a few years later, she joined her husband. What would have happened to Mr. and Mrs. Aune if my dad had responded to her in a harsh way that summer afternoon? Instead, God used a soft answer, a kind word, a loving deed, a blessing, to expand His kingdom here on earth.[5]

"DADDY . . . IS THAT YOU?"

Becky's story as told to Ken Sande

God can do anything, you know—far more than you could

ever imagine or guess or request in your wildest dreams!

EPHESIANS 3:20 MSG

I looked forward to my wedding with a mixture of excitement and sadness. Mark was the man of my dreams, and I was thrilled about becoming his wife. But there was another man who was in my thoughts more often than Mark, and the memory of him brought mostly pain.

My father, Frank, abandoned our family when I was only five years old. Week after week, I longed to see him, to feel his strong hugs, and to tell him how much I wanted him to come home. But he could hardly bear the pain of such visits, so I saw little of him for nearly twenty years. As time passed, my loneliness mingled with bitterness and a fear of getting too close to others who might also abandon me.

I shared these feelings with my pastor and Mark during premarital counseling. Drawing on reconciliation principles from Peacemaker® Ministries,⁶ Pastor Hall helped me to take some of the things that could cast a shadow over our marriage to the Lord. But he knew that there was another step that would help me to lay the past completely to rest.

Two weeks before the wedding, Pastor Hall passed through the city where I believed my father lived. With some trepidation, he found my father's name in the telephone book and called him. To his surprise, my father agreed to meet him for lunch.

As the two men talked, Pastor Hall realized that, even though my father was not a Christian, the Holy Spirit had been working in his heart to prepare him for their meeting. Sensing this, Pastor Hall said, "Wouldn't this be an ideal time to seek reconciliation with Becky?"

Pastor Hall prayed silently as my father wrestled with hope and fear. The Holy Spirit gave my father grace, and he asked for my telephone number.

That evening, my father dialed my number with trembling hands. When I answered, he said, "Hello, Becky. This is your dad."

After a few moments, I said something that he had not heard for years.

"Daddy . . . is that you?"

The eagerness in my voice must have swept away his fears, because he began telling me how much he missed me and asked me to forgive him for what he had done. God filled my heart with love and forgiveness, and we were reconciled in a flood of words and tears.

As the conversation neared its end, I said, "Daddy, I'm getting married in two weeks! Could you come and give me away?"

"Of course!" he said. "I want very much to meet your Mark."

After I hung up the phone, I suddenly realized what I had done. How would my mother, my stepfather, and my brothers and sisters react to my father? Had I just ruined my own wedding? I poured out my heart to the Lord in thanksgiving and need.

In the following days, Mark and Pastor Hall reminded me of God's faithfulness and pointed out that He was obviously working in the situation. Together, we prepared the rest of my family to receive Dad.

When the weekend of the wedding finally arrived, everyone was nervous about the unusual reunion. There were several awkward moments, but we made it through the rehearsal and wedding without incident.

All day long, God had been working in my dad to give him the courage to do something he had not planned to do. During the reception, he stood up and cleared his throat. Raising his glass toward my mother, he said, "I want to propose a toast to Susan for her faith, endurance, and character and for the wonderful job she did in raising our children."

He lowered his glass and looked around the room. Then he continued, "I also want to ask forgiveness for all of the pain I've caused so many of you through my selfish actions."

Finally he lifted his glass high and said, "Most of all, I want to thank God that my daughter is marrying a Christian and that her pastor loves her enough to reach out to me."

There was not a dry eye in the room as I ran into my father's arms, thanking him for the best wedding gift he could ever have given me. Other family members went to him as well, expressing their forgiveness and pushing aside the walls that had divided our family for twenty years.

But God's greatest blessing was yet to come.

The most important reconciliation took place a month later when Pastor Hall called my dad to ask how he was doing. God had continued to work in Dad's heart, and he wanted to hear more about the Person who had restored him to his family. After hearing what Jesus had done for him on the cross, my dad eagerly confessed his sin and put his faith in Jesus Christ.

When I heard the news, I knew that the reconciliation process was complete. By God's grace, my father and I will never be separated again.[7]

"BUT GOD, I DON'T WANT TO FORGIVE THEM"

by Karen Hardin

If it is possible, as far as it depends on you,

live at peace with everyone.

ROMANS 12:18

Some things are just easier to love and appreciate than others. Take chocolate or warm, fuzzy kittens; a beautiful sunset or a crisp October sky. Some things hold an almost universal appeal, although it might be difficult to explain why. On the other hand, there are things that can repel us just as strongly. Unfortunately, that sometimes includes people.

It's easy to love people who agree with us, think like we do, and love us. That's a given. But the command to "love thy neighbor" comes without conditions. No one ever said it was going to be easy . . . but it is mandatory.

My husband, Kevin, and I first met Dave and Kelly when we were placed together on an overseas ministry outreach team, meaning that we would work closely with them for the next six years. We shared a zeal to communicate the love of Christ to those who had never heard the gospel. And that was about the only thing we had in common.

This couple was about as loveable and cuddly as a porcupine poised for attack. But then again, they probably felt the same about us. It might not have been a problem had we not been assigned lodging on the same floor of an apartment complex consisting of only three apartments—theirs, ours, and another couple's—making frequent contact unavoidable. Not to mention that after a season, Kevin and I were put into a leadership capacity over the ministry outreach team. This new development seemed to add insult to injury for Dave and Kelly, who were approximately ten years our senior. From that point on, the relationship made a speedy descent.

"Honey, it's impossible," I sighed in frustration on more than one occasion as Kevin and I discussed the situation. "It doesn't matter what I say, Kelly disagrees with me. It's like she's just looking for a fight."

"It can't be that bad," my husband—the perpetual peacemaker—consoled.

But it was.

Not long after, as our team went on a short-term outreach to a different area, I decided to test my theory. Overhearing Kelly's conversation with another teammate, I learned of her interest in a specific type of music. She said she felt a sense of comfort and nostalgia each time she heard specific songs.

Later in the day, as Kelly and I found ourselves seated across from each other, I made another stab at friendship.

Keep it even, I reminded myself, mentally walking on eggshells as I worked at making acceptable conversation. A few minutes of pleasantries were exchanged before I brought the conversation around to music. Having overheard Kelly's preference, I felt I was finally in safe waters.

Turning the comment that I had overheard into a question,

I asked, "Don't you sometimes miss the music we grew up with?"

I was shocked when Kelly leveled her gaze at me and took aim. "No, I have completely adjusted to our new ministry environment and don't really miss anything. Besides, music isn't what is supposed to bring us comfort in the first place."

Another conversation derailed.

No, it really didn't seem to matter what Kevin or I said to this couple as they repeatedly let us know their disdain for us. Living in peace with them seemed a fleeting hope. But we didn't give up.

We tried various forms of reconciliation. We invited them over for dinner. I made soup for them when they were ill. We even helped them replace their bikes when they were stolen—not once, but twice. Nothing we did seemed to smooth the turbulent waters between us.

From time to time, I even learned of comments they had made about us to others in the form of "prayer requests." These often became ugly rumors that circulated, undermining the effectiveness of our leadership within the group.

In all fairness, Kevin and I were far from perfect. Young in our leadership skills, we made numerous mistakes with the team as a whole, not to mention our dealings with Dave and Kelly. I certainly had to make frequent attitude adjustments and learn to keep my mouth shut. There were many times when I wanted to retaliate against their constant stealthy attacks and to defend myself before my attackers, but I knew this would only prolong the war. Our attempts to talk with them about areas of disagreement were simply ignored.

Returning to our apartment one afternoon, I found a note

taped to the door. I unlocked the door, placed my packages on the table, and began to read—the words left me stunned.

In the note, Dave and Kelly had made a list of grievances against us—these issues covered a range of topics from how we ministered and how we dressed to conversations we had engaged in. The letter was three pages long and included numbered offenses, the majority of which had taken place when neither Dave nor Kelly had been present. The only way they could have heard about the situations was through word of mouth. The letter contained very little truth.

My first reaction was a swelling anger as I felt heat flood my face. *How dare they piously accuse us of things they have no real facts about!* I thought. Not to mention that they were obviously unwilling to address their concerns face-to-face in a biblical manner.

Fortunately, within moments, I sensed the Holy Spirit speak to my heart. *Forgive.*

I knew it had to be God's prompting because that was about the last thing in my heart at that particular moment. I took a deep breath, and as I did, I knew it was right. This had to stop somewhere.

I prayed for several minutes before taking pen and paper to respond to each and every grievance Dave and Kelly had listed. Instead of defending ourselves, I simply apologized to them, slowly working my way through the pages, addressing each attack with an apology and sometimes sharing a few of the details they may not have heard about. After completing the note, I reread it to make sure it was free of any animosity or defensiveness. In that moment, I understood that it really didn't matter what Dave and Kelly thought about us, as long as Kevin and I were able to walk in love and forgiveness . . . regardless of their response. I folded the letter and put it into an envelope, then walked across the hall to their apartment and taped my response to their door.

And I prayed.

When Kevin returned that afternoon, I shared with him what had transpired regarding the letter, the accusations, and my response. His anger initially flared the same way mine had, but I watched as almost immediately that same supernatural peace flooded over him as well. We chose to let it go.

The next day after lunch, there was a knock at the door. I was more than surprised to see Kelly standing there with the letter in her hand. "I am so sorry," she began, embarrassment evident on her face. "We obviously didn't have all the facts. Will you please forgive us?"

There were many tears that day as we joined together in prayer, choosing to work together on the difficult relationship. And while I can't say that the relationship was always perfect after that day, I can say that God's love and forgiveness was.[8]

GET THE LOG OUT

by Ed Gungor

Jesus said, "Why do you look at the speck that is in your

brother's eye, but do not notice the log that is in your own eye?

Or how can you say to your brother, 'Let me take the speck

out of your eye,' and behold, the log is in your own eye?

You hypocrite, first take the log out of your own eye,

and then you will see clearly to take the speck

out of your brother's eye."

MATTHEW 7:3-5 NASB

While my wife, Gail, and I were attending Bible school, we met one of the nicest people we have ever met. Bill was a caring and trusted friend. The only real problem we had with him was that he did not carry his own weight financially. He would continually ask us for rides home, borrow our car, use our phone, eat our meals, or come over to our apartment on hot summer days to keep from having to turn on his air conditioner. You get the picture.

At first it didn't bother me. I grew up in a home where we always shared what we had with others. But over time, I began to resent the fact that Bill never even offered to chip in for the expenses that he had helped to incur.

By our second year of school, the situation was getting old. Every time I looked at Bill, it reminded me that he was using us. I knew that if I spoke to him about the problem while I was upset, it would have really hurt him. So I kept quiet, avoiding him at school and leaving the room when he visited our apartment.

At one point I commented to Gail, "He is getting on my nerves so much; I feel like punching him!"

She told me I had better deal with my feelings before I said something I would regret—so I finally made it a matter of prayer.

A few days later, as I was exiting a freeway ramp, I heard God speak inside me, *You're making his splinter a log.*

"What?" I asked.

You're making his splinter a log, He repeated.

I was driving with my eyes wide open, and at the same time, clearly viewing a mini-movie inside my head. I saw our friend Bill, who had become "the cheapskate" in my mind, with what looked like a little thorn sticking out of his eye. As I lifted my hand to the thorn, an exact duplicate appeared between my thumb and index finger. In this inner vision, I saw myself taking the duplicate splinter and bringing it so close to my face that all I saw was the splinter—and it became so large that it had become a log!

The Lord was trying to show me that I had lost sight of the fact that Bill was a precious brother with a problem—a splinter. Instead, in my eyes, he had actually become the problem—a log.

The Lord reminded me of the verse in Matthew 7 that said if I wanted to help Bill, then I would have to "first take the log out of [my] own eye, and then [I would] see clearly to take the speck out of [my] brother's eye" (v. 5 NASB).

The next day when I saw Bill, I saw him in a different way. I now saw him as a precious brother with a problem, instead of a problem brother. That is when I knew I could speak with him without being judgmental and without hurting him. So I decided to approach him.

But before I could say a word, Bill said, "Ed, God began dealing with me yesterday about taking advantage of you and Gail. I need to be more responsible . . . Please take this twenty dollars as a start. I'm really sorry."

To forgive Bill, I had to separate him from his sin. This separation opened the door for a change to come—in both of us! Forgiving and releasing Bill from his sin was God's way of bringing restoration. It also set the stage for the necessary change to take place in him. By not forgiving Bill, I had hindered God from touching him through me. God was gracious to show me the situation through his eyes so that I could forgive. Forgiveness allowed the log to become a splinter again; and then, God even removed the splinter itself.

Not in Vain

by Peggy Littell as told to Kayleen J. Reusser

Be steadfast, immovable, always abounding in the work of the

Lord, knowing that your labor is not in vain in the Lord.

1 Corinthians 15:58 nkjv

The news of my husband's death immobilized me. Matt had been riding a moped in downtown Cagayan de Oro in the Philippines, where we were missionaries, when a bus driver failed to see him, veered out of traffic, and hit him.

Although our pain was excruciating, our church family surrounded us with love and support. One way they do this in the Philippines is to hold "services of hope" whenever a church member dies. These meetings are held each night preceding the funeral and blend evangelistic and memorial services with a time of singing.

While I was standing at the first service of hope, a thought came to me. Of all the people who had been affected by Matt's death, one had been forgotten—the driver of the bus.

Philippine law states that if someone causes another person's death, then the guilty party is jailed until the matter is fully investigated. However, according to the law, the prisoner will be released at the request of the victim's family. I spoke with one of the church leaders who volunteered to go to the prison and sign papers stating that I wanted the driver to be released.

The next night at the service, more people came to express their condolences, including a man with his head held low as he approached me. Without saying a word, he took my hand and held it tightly as tears streamed down his face. I knew that he was the driver of the bus that had killed Matt.

With the help of a church member, who knew several dialects, I told the driver that I did not hold him accountable for Matt's death and that I was happy for his release from prison.

The driver's eyes widened. His lips parted in a smile so brilliant that I couldn't help smiling back. "My husband was a Christian," I explained. "He loved the Filipino people so much that he chose to live here to tell them about God's love. Would you like to learn more about God's love and forgiveness?"

The man shook his head and then left the church. I didn't expect to see him again; but the next night, at the last service of hope, he approached me, this time accompanied by his wife and three sisters. All four women cried noisily on my shoulder, grateful for their loved one's release from prison.

The driver and his family also attended the funeral. Matt's parents told him that they, too, forgave him for Matt's death and believed that God would somehow bring good out of it.

To our great joy, the driver and his family began attending church regularly, bringing a bus filled with people from his barrio.

Only the Lord Jesus could take a vessel that had brought death—like that bus—and use it to bring people to himself, I thought.

When the driver and his family eventually accepted Jesus Christ into their lives, I praised God and knew that in heaven Matt was praising God, too—right along with all the angels.

Forgiveness is man's deepest need

and highest achievement.

HORACE BUSHNELL

Forgiving Others

⎯⎯⎯ ⌘ ⎯⎯⎯

Peter came to Him and said, "Lord, how often shall my

brother sin against me, and I forgive him? Up to seven times?"

Jesus said to him, "I do not say to you, up to seven times,

but up to seventy times seven."

MATTHEW 18:21-22 NKJV

There once was a teacher who wanted to illustrate the
effects of unforgiveness on those who possess it. So as part of
an assignment, the teacher assigned a group of students to
bring a clear plastic bag and a sack of potatoes to school. For
every person the students had refused to forgive throughout
their lives, they were to choose a potato and put it into the
plastic bag. Then they were to carry this bag with them everywhere they went for one week. They were to take it to class,
have it on the car seat next to them while driving, put it beside
their beds at night, and take it with them to the movies. Everywhere they went, the potatoes went, too.

Well, as you can imagine, some students had very heavy
bags. But even the bags with only one or two potatoes became
a nuisance after a while. The students were embarrassed to
carry the bag of potatoes around in public, and their friends

were embarrassed to be seen with them. The heavy sack made carrying their books more difficult. As the week wore on, not only were the potatoes a burden, they began to grow horns and break down into a slimy, smelly mess. The students got the point.[9]

You may think that a little grudge doesn't really affect you, but are you sure? Actually, we pay a high price when we lug around emotional baggage. It hinders us and gets in our way. A grudge can cause us to behave in embarrassing ways and become a nuisance. Instead of our lives bearing the sweet savor of Christ, our attitudes can get downright stinky. Some might even say that we have grown horns! James said it this way: "Where envying and strife is, there is confusion and *every evil work*" (James 3:16 KJV, emphasis added).

Doctors claim that many illnesses are linked to negative emotions. Have you ever heard the phrase, "What's eating you?" If you are harboring bitterness, then that may be more than just a figure of speech. It may be a contributing factor to sleep and eating disorders, neck and back pain (e.g., "a pain in the neck"), digestive problems, ulcers, high blood pressure, headaches, arthritis. Even cancer may have an emotional component that is eating away at your well-being. Bitterness is like drinking poison and hoping the other person gets sick! Nothing will lock you up and zap your energy like nursing old wounds and coddling unforgiveness. It's like harboring a personal terrorist bent on your destruction.

It's important to note that the price for unforgiveness includes more than just your health and happiness. It means being unforgiven yourself. It is a strong and difficult truth; yet the Bible is clear: "If you do not forgive, neither will your

Father in heaven forgive your trespasses" (Mark 11:26 NKJV).

Sure, you may have been hurt, treated unfairly, abused, neglected, humiliated, persecuted, or lied about. We don't possess emotional baggage without a significant cause. Your anger may be understandable or even justified. But are you willing to pay the high price for hanging on to it?

It's true; forgiveness rarely comes easily. Sometimes we have to forgive over and over again—seventy times seven if necessary. And the journey is not always a straight one. More likely the pilgrimage is filled with stops and starts, gloomy and sunny days, and many steps forward and backward before achieving the freedom and peace that forgiveness brings.

No, we can't always control the things that happen to us, but we can choose how we handle them. It may sound trite, but forgiveness begins with a decision—a decision to not dwell on what happened. It means that you are willing to dismiss negative thoughts about the one who wronged you, to not seek revenge or even wish that person ill.

Sometimes we have to forgive through gritted teeth—but the more often we decide to forgive, the easier it becomes. Plus, God is there to help you. If you will make the decision to begin forgiving, then He will give you the grace and strength to walk it out. Don't be surprised or discouraged when negative emotions seem to stick to you like flypaper; they are indeed persistent. But if you will abide close to God and dwell on the good things in His Word, you will reach the point—by God's grace— where you can truly let go.

Many others have walked the difficult path of forgiveness. You will read some of their stories in the pages that follow. They will encourage you and give you hope. The characters and circumstances might be different from your own; but you will find a common thread—that forgiveness sets you free. These stories reveal how people can navigate through their pain and, with God's help, find the grace to forgive. Many of these stories demonstrate that when a person finally comes to the place of letting go, they are flooded with the peace of God. The people in these stories are lighter, more hopeful, and energized after choosing to forgive. This is the life God wants for us—it's what He wants for you.

As you walk through the pages that follow, let God take you by the hand. And don't forget to dump your "potatoes" as you go.

SWEET SURRENDER

by Karen O'Connor

God is working in you, giving you the desire to obey him and

the power to do what pleases him.

PHILIPPIANS 2:13 NLT

I thought about her. I dreamed about her. I saw her in every woman I met. Some had her name—Cathy. Others had her deep-set blue eyes or her curly dark hair. Even the slightest resemblance tied my stomach into a knot.

I felt trapped with my thoughts. Weeks, months, and years passed. Would I ever be free of the woman who had gone after my husband and ultimately married him? I couldn't go on like this. The endless rage, resentment, guilt, and anger drained the life out of everything I did. I went into counseling. I attended self-help classes, seminars, and workshops. I read books. I talked to anyone who would listen.

I ran. I walked the beach. I drove for miles going nowhere. I screamed into my pillow at night. I meditated. I prayed. I blamed myself. I did everything I knew how to do—except surrender.

Then one Saturday in 1982, I went to a day-long seminar on the healing power of forgiveness sponsored by a church in my neighborhood. After some discussion and sharing, participants were asked to close their eyes and locate someone in their lives they had not forgiven—for whatever reason, real or imagined.

Next, the leader invited us to look at whether or not we would be willing to forgive that person. Naturally, my first thought was Cathy. My stomach churned again. My hands were suddenly wet, and my head throbbed. I felt I had to get out of that room, but something kept me in my seat.

How could I forgive a person like Cathy? She had not only hurt me—she had hurt my children, too. So I turned my attention to other people in my life—my mother. She'd be easy to forgive. I could possibly forgive my friend Ann or my former high-school English teacher—anyone but Cathy. But there was no escape. The name persisted, and her face grew large in my mind.

Then a voice within gently asked, *Are you ready to let go of this? Can you release her and forgive yourself, as well?*

I turned hot, then cold. I began to shake. I was certain everyone around me could hear my heart beating. Yes, I was willing. I couldn't hold on to my anger any longer. It was killing me. In that moment, without doing anything else, an incredible shift took place in my heart. I simply let go!

I can't describe it. I don't know what happened or what prompted me to do the very thing that I had resisted so doggedly for months. All I know is that for the first time in four years, I completely surrendered to the Holy Spirit. I released my grip on Cathy, on my ex-husband, and on myself. I let go of the anger—just like that.

Within seconds, energy rushed through every cell of my body. My mind became alert; my heart lightened. I saw things I had not seen before. Suddenly I realized that as long as I separated myself from even one person, I separated myself from God.

How "righteous" I had been. How arrogant and possessive.

How important it had been for me to be right, no matter what the cost. And it had cost me plenty—my health, my spontaneity, my joy in living.

I had no idea what was next, but it didn't matter. That night I slept straight through till morning. No dreams. No haunting face. No reminders.

If it had been up to me alone, I don't know if I would have had the courage or the generosity to make the first move. But it was not up to me. There was no mistaking the power of the Holy Spirit within me.

The following Monday, I walked into my office and wrote a letter to Cathy. The words spilled onto the page without effort.

"Dear Cathy," I began, "On Saturday morning . . ." and I proceeded to tell her what had occurred.

I told her how I had deliberately continued to separate myself from her—to judge her for what she had done; and as a result, how I had denied both of us the healing power of forgiveness.

On Wednesday afternoon of the same week, the phone rang.

"Karen?"

There was no mistaking the voice.

"It's Cathy," she said softly.

Surprisingly my stomach remained calm. My hands were dry. My voice was steady and sure. I listened more than I talked—unusual for me. I found myself actually interested in what Cathy had to say.

She thanked me for the letter and acknowledged my courage in writing it. Then she told me how sorry she was—for everything. She talked briefly about her regret, her sadness for me, and more. All I had wanted to hear from her, she said that day.

As I replaced the receiver, however, I realized that as nice as it was to hear her words of apology, they didn't really matter. They paled in comparison to what God was teaching me. Buried deep in the trauma of my divorce was the truth I had been looking for all my life without even knowing it: God is my source, my strength, and my very supply. He alone can minister healing.

For four years I had been caught in the externals, the reasons, the lies, the excuses, the jealousy, and the anger. But now I had experienced the freedom that had previously only been a stack of psychological insights. Now I really knew that no one can keep me in bondage as long as I am in God's hands. No one can rob me of my joy—unless I allow them to.

My life belongs to God and every experience—no matter how painful or confusing it seems—can aid in my spiritual growth. Every moment has a purpose if I am serving the Lord.

Since then I have started over again in another city—free of the jealousy, anger, and resentment that bound me. I am free to enjoy all the wonderful experiences that God has for me. "'For I know the plans I have for you,' declares the LORD, 'plans to prosper you and not to harm you, plans to give you hope and a future'" (Jeremiah 29:11-12).

God wants to be our leverage in living, empowering us to feel better about ourselves, more excited about our future, more grateful for those we love, and more enthusiastic about our faith. God has given us His Holy Spirit to help us live according to His perfect plan. As we surrender to Him, we will be truly free.

AN IMPOSSIBLE GIFT

by John Howard Prin

Jesus said, "Without God, it is utterly impossible. But with God everything is possible."

MARK 10:27 TLB

My wife enjoys telling folks, "John went to Hollywood to get an Oscar, but he got Jesus instead." In one simple sentence, she explains what happened after seven frustrating years in Tinseltown when, at the age of thirty-three, I despaired of my dream ever coming true. Instead of glory, I reaped nail-biting angst and drug addiction until suicide seemed the only way to end my misery. Then, alone in a stranger's wheat field on a chilly November day, I begged Jesus to save me from my wretched reality. To my amazement, at that very moment Jesus became real to me, and His everlasting arms engulfed me in a loving embrace that remains today, twenty-five years later.

One sunny afternoon six months after my conversion, I was walking on the hillside below the famous H-O-L-L-Y-W-O-O-D sign and struggling to discern the Lord's new direction for my career. On the secluded footpath, just below those twenty-foot-high letters, I felt a sudden supernatural nudge. *Forgive your mother.* I stopped, wondering if I was hearing things. The inner nudge came again. *Forgive your mother.* I couldn't fathom such a thing because of my extreme hatred of her. As I kept walking, the nudge came a third time. *Forgive your mother.*

Finally, I stopped, sat down in the dirt, and began arguing with God. In the next few seconds, a tidal wave of reasons why she did not deserve forgiveness flooded my mind.

Ugly memories erupted.

I recalled the selfish, tyrannical demands she made on us kids while our dad was dying from diabetes. After my dad's right leg was amputated in 1957, my twin brother, Dave, and I, just thirteen years old, began rotating the duty of sleeping beside Dad while Mom retreated to another bedroom. She couldn't handle Dad's condition. This left us alone to help Dad hobble to the bathroom in the middle of the night, wrap the stump of his sawed-off leg with fresh bandages, and fill his glass with water for pain pills.

Meanwhile my mother began to obsess even more over her grandiose dreams of living high in our huge lakeshore house. This meant relentless decorating and landscaping projects for my brothers and me—and amounted to nothing short of slavery. Homework and after-school activities took a back seat to her projects. Once she made us move an entire grove of birch trees some three hundred yards just so she could enjoy viewing them. Then there was our fourteenth birthday—our party was ruined when she insisted that we haul dozens of heavy paving stones in 100-degree heat, to build a patio.

Sitting there on the dusty path in Hollywood, I rattled off these anguished memories to God as evidence that forgiveness was impossible. Then, suddenly, the essence of a recent devotional reading popped into my mind: "If anyone has a complaint against another, forgive each other; just as the Lord has forgiven you, so you also must forgive" (Colossians 3:13 NRSV).

"NO!" I shouted aloud. "NO, NO, NO!"

Silence.

The nudge came again. *Forgive your mother.*

"Impossible!" I blurted out. The same hatred I'd felt years earlier kindled within me as I recalled her decorating projects, which typically entailed countless hours of toil for her children. Another example is the time she made us tile the entire ground floor of our spacious house. This task meant covering 1,600 square feet with one-foot-square linoleum tiles so that she could save money. My brothers and I stared at the concrete floor, the boxes of brown floor tiles, and the five-gallon bucket of black, sticky glue. We had no experience, but we knew she expected professional results.

Even meals were difficult. We chafed at having to cook our own food and always meeting her needs—and Dad's—before our own. Behind her back, we grumbled about her arrogant sense of entitlement.

Then another memory surfaced. I had just stepped off the school bus and was heading home one afternoon when I began to have murderous thoughts. *Take a kitchen knife and do her in.* I rejected the idea instantly; the thought alarmed and appalled me. But it stubbornly returned. My gut churned, my pulse raced, and my breathing doubled. *What if I did kill her? No, impossible!* I tried, but I couldn't shake the thought. I was relieved to find she wasn't home. But that night I heard her return and laid in bed, terrified of my thoughts, fearful that I would act on them. Thank God, I never did.

The fury I harbored—especially the struggle to reconcile the thoughts of killing Mom with my genuine love for her—

had tormented me for twelve long years. Now here I was with God's still small voice whispering, *Forgive your mother.*

"No!" I stood up, kicked the dirt, and stubbornly hiked on. For the next couple of weeks, I held a running debate with God. Feeling the pressure to obey, I brought up every argument I could think of: Mom did not deserve forgiveness; she made Dad so miserable that he died at fifty-nine. If she came begging, then maybe I would consider forgiving her. But she hadn't done that.

In time, my thoughts shifted to the things for which I had been forgiven. It was a long list. Finally, I returned to the spot near the sign, knelt, and stammered aloud, "Mom, I-I forgive you."

Sobs welled up in my chest, and tears poured out onto my face. "I-I do forgive you, Mom, from my heart, truly." Waves of sorrow and grief dislodged and floated away from me. My entire body shook and trembled.

As the tears subsided, I stood, feeling freer than I had ever felt as an adult. Mom no longer was the focus of my pain. I no longer viewed her as the villain, but more like the mother she had been when I was a small child. I no longer imagined her scowling, but smiling and caring.

In the months and seasons ahead, the same gentle nudge repeated itself over and over, triggering specific memories. Each time I struggled to let go, presenting my arguments to God in prayer. But in every instance, His love trumped my resistance, and I managed to obey "the nudge" more and more easily. Each time I forgave Mom, another old hurt faded and lost its power.

Eventually, I flew to my hometown in Minnesota during the Christmas holidays with my wife, Susie, and daughter,

Emily, to visit my mom and brothers. Except for occasional phone calls or birthday cards, little communication had occurred between Mom and me for more than fifteen years. I'll never forget how Mom greeted us with her best manners and a big smile.

"Merry Christmas!" she chimed, greeting Emily first, and then Susie. Turning to me, she stared at my face and cried out, "Johnny, you've changed! You look so happy! What's happened?"

I smiled. "Yes, Mom, I've changed. I love you."

Abruptly, her hands flew up to her face and she gasped. "You're the first of my sons to tell me that in years and years." Letting her hands down to look again, she reached for me, and I could see tears wetting her cheeks. "You love me? Really?"

I nodded. "Yes, Mom. I've forgiven you."

Awestruck, she replied, "Forgiven me? For what?"

Right then, with ham baking in the oven and potatoes simmering on the stove, we hugged and walked to the den where we sat privately. For the next forty-five minutes, I told Mom about how horribly oppressive those years had been to me and the many times I'd felt hurt and abused.

She listened and muttered, "I'm sorry," and, "I had no idea." For the first time since I was a young boy, I sensed that she really heard me and wanted to understand me. Tears flowed down her cheeks.

Something good was taking place. Something that I'd considered impossible in this lifetime was miraculously happening. In the days ahead, as we celebrated the Birthday of birthdays, we exchanged gifts that included more than just those under the tree.[10]

A FINAL REUNION

by Dee Smith

Love covers a multitude of sins.

1 PETER 4:8 NASB

My journey of deliverance from hate is an amazing story of God's sovereignty and patience. Bitterness flooded my heart for years. The root of bitterness became embedded after six years of my father's intense, unremitting abuse. My memories of childhood were wiped out except for fragments, nightmares, and unexplainable attacks of panic. I felt haunted and stalked by evil. Was I beyond God's reach? I thought so; but one sunny afternoon in a hospital room, I learned about forgiveness. Love and mercy triumphed over hatred and vengeance. My father and I reconciled just before he died. How this happened demonstrates God's power and love.

I was a young mother of two before suppressed memories of my father's abuse surfaced in vivid, shocking detail. But I refused to deal with them and told no one. Instead I blamed God for allowing such a horrible thing to happen to a child. For ten years I stopped praying, reading the Bible, and attending church. I chose to cut off all communication with my father and the rest of my family. I refused their phone calls, returned their letters, and made certain they knew nothing about my life.

What I didn't know during those unhappy years was that

someone was praying for me every day. That "someone" was my aunt. When my mother abandoned me and my father was serving in World War II, she stepped forward to raise me. She was also the person who taught me about Jesus.

As a result of my aunt's prayers, God provided a miracle. My father had returned to his family after years of alcoholism and restlessness, which compelled him to wander the globe. His brothers and their grown children took him in and cared for him when he was penniless, homeless, and dying. My father's final request was to see his daughter.

My aunt doggedly called every Smith listed in the Houston telephone directory, the last address they knew for me. Persistence paid off. I was surprised but not shocked by the news. For months I had been plagued by a sense of urgency to search for my father.

I flew immediately to Reno, Nevada, where my dad was hospitalized. Once in flight, I had two hours alone with my thoughts. Reading was impossible—so was sleep—and I couldn't tell the pilot to turn around. Thoughts replayed in my head: *So, he's dying. So what? How am I supposed to feel after what he did to me fourteen years ago?*

The following afternoon, I went to see my father. It was time to bid good-bye. I wondered what we would say. Would we talk about something pointless and mundane? Would I lash out in anger? Would he admit what he'd done and beg me to forgive him? Or would he call me a liar and a crazy woman? I had no script.

I found the room, but it took awhile for me to enter. Scared to death, I wanted to run away. Finally, I prayed for courage and pushed the door open. I couldn't hold back a gasp. *This feeble old man is my father?* I thought. The person carved in my memory was handsome, broad shouldered, and strong—the man who terrified me by night and treasured me by day.

I had the feeling that I was in the wrong room. But then, he spoke my name and stretched out his arms. I grasped his hands and helped him into a wheelchair parked nearby. I was reassured when I could finally look into his eyes. They were the same color as mine—hazel—and they had the twinkle that I remembered as a little girl.

"Hi, baby. It's good to see you," he said.

I knew about the devastating physical changes caused by the cancer, but reality was still pretty hard to take. Cancer of the jaw had resulted in the removal of part of his jawbone. Most of the left side of his face looked caved in; his mouth and the tissue around his left eye twisted downward. The loss of bone, skin, and muscle had ruined his ability to smile or achieve any expression on that side. He smiled, chewed, spoke, or moved his face only on the right side. His weight loss was so dramatic that his shirt and pants looked like clothes hung on a clothesline.

I stammered, "Where do you want me to take you?"

He directed me to a secluded snack bar at the end of his floor. He was alert, although quite weak, and explained that he wanted to be somewhere we wouldn't be interrupted. Once settled in the snack bar, our conversation flowed naturally. We talked about the happy times we had shared together when I was very young. He was not an educated man, but I loved the gift he had for describing in poetic language his appreciation of God's beautiful scenery. He had enjoyed finding out about the other cultures that lived in the exotic countries where he had traveled as a seaman. He loved seagulls, and I remembered how he had described many different species found throughout the world.

I asked, "Do you remember any of the stories you wrote in your letters from New Guinea when you were a soldier? I was a little girl then, but I remember. My favorite was how the coconuts got their eyes."

He hesitated for a moment before telling the story just as I remembered it. Then he followed it up with a couple more that I had forgotten. We laughed together when I told him the stories were always a hit when I shared them at show-and-tell in the second grade.

An hour later, I hurried him back to his room because he looked like he was in a lot of pain and very tired. Orderlies assisted him into bed while I found a nurse to bring something for his pain. I knew he would fall asleep soon after the injection and our time together was almost over. Seeing him suffer and listening to his promise that he'd "get well and head out for Texas" to meet his grandchildren touched something deep inside of me. It was love. It was a desire to comfort and care for him.

After everyone left, peace engulfed the room. I found a hairbrush and brushed his hair. It was still thick and curly, but the dark hair was white now. I cooled his face and neck with a washrag—I think I even sang his favorite song, "Trees." I sang it on pitch. When I was a kid, he'd sing it at the top of his lungs. He sang so off-key that everyone in the vicinity groaned. As I brushed, I told him about his grandchildren.

I felt tears streaming down my cheeks as I watched him slip into sleep. I placed my cheek against his good cheek and said, "Good-bye, Daddy. I love you. You're a good father to me." As

I spoke, he opened his eyes and looked steadily into mine. He didn't speak, but in his eyes I saw peace—peace anchored in the knowledge that I had forgiven him and a certainty that God had forgiven him. I laid my head on his chest to feel his heartbeat and cry for the man I had hated and feared most of my life. Within minutes, he fell asleep again, and our visit was over.

Words are inadequate to explain the power of those last hours we had together. I learned from an uncle that God had miraculously brought my father to the point of accepting Christ. Then, He had enabled me to be there at the end to tell him that I loved him. Through my words and tears, I was finally able to release and forgive him completely. My dad would be waiting for me in Paradise—and that was the Lord's gift to me.

Years later, I stood in front of a small square stone embedded in the grass at the veteran's cemetery in White City, Oregon. It was not much of a memorial, but it marked the life of a man who was important to me—a son, a brother, a father, and a soldier who had served his country honorably.

The cemetery was a beautiful place, facing a mountain range. Beyond the mountains was the sea he loved. I was finally ready to confront him with what I needed to say. I read aloud a letter pouring out my pain and suffering at his hands. Then I prayed for God to forgive me for my years of bitter hatred for this man. As the breeze gently touched my face, I finally knew that all was well.

CALMING THE STORM

by Janet Eckles

They cried out to the LORD in their trouble, and he brought

them out of their distress. He stilled the storm to a whisper; the

waves of the sea were hushed.

PSALM 107:28-29

"The jury has reached its verdict," announced the bailiff as he swung open the large courtroom doors. This brought about an instant hush from the crowd in the hallway.

It took the jury three hours to arrive at their decision— three hours that seemed like days to me.

I gripped my husband's hand as we shuffled into the courtroom ahead of our two sons and the rest of our family and friends. Sitting stiffly on the hard benches, no one spoke.

"Rise," announced the bailiff with authority.

I held my breath. My heart beat with force. We were about to hear the verdict. *Finally, we'll see justice done!* I thought.

The phone rang early on that day more than a year ago— September 7, 2002, around 2:30 A.M. In moments, our middle son, Jeff, raced into our bedroom shouting, "Joe's been hurt!" We frantically pulled on our clothes from the day before and rushed out the door. We arrived at the hospital minutes after

the ambulance, but we received only one small piece of information: "They're working on him."

This isn't happening to us! I thought with anguished disbelief. Once in the emergency room, however, we received the
heart-wrenching news. Joe had not survived the multiple stab
wounds inflicted on his body.

I crumpled to the floor, sick with grief.

"These things don't happen to good boys!" I wanted to
shout. The light of my life had been snuffed out, and I was
being buffeted by winds of unbearable pain.

God's Word became my anchor. "Be still, and know that I
am God" (Psalm 46:10) echoed in my heart over and over
again. His Word sounded loud and clear: "My grace is sufficient for you" (2 Corinthians 12:9 RSV).

God's grace was precisely what sustained me during the
excruciating pain of losing Joe. A year crawled by, as I
reviewed the precious memories of each season of his life—the
spring of Joe's vibrant personality; the summer of his loving
hugs and kisses; the fall of the remarkable changes as the
teenager emerged from the small boy; and finally the winter,
bringing with it the cruel and bitter coldness of his death.

The trial was scheduled to begin on October 27. Ironically,
it was my fifty-first birthday.

"I'm not sure I'm ready," I confessed to my husband.

"I'm not sure, either, but we need to know what happened," he replied with a pained sigh.

The trial began. Each witness was called to relate their side
of the story. What began as an exchange of words between the
drivers of two cars had turned into an angry confrontation in a
parking lot. As they fought, the other man pulled a knife and

stabbed our Joe twenty-three times.

Help me, God! my heart cried out. *I don't know if I can bear one more detail of that dreadful night!*

But the torture continued.

The medical examiner's report of Joe's stab wounds was unbearable.

After we listened to all the witnesses, the judge instructed the jury.

"Have you reached a verdict?" he asked.

"We have," answered the foreman of the jury.

I held my breath as the foreman read the three counts. Later, the only words I could remember hearing were, "Not guilty on all counts." A gasp of horror burst from our side of the courtroom. I heard sobbing and cries from the other side. They were relieved by the acquittal; and we were horrified by the injustice. The jury had believed the defendant's plea of self-defense.

"This is impossible for me. Be my rock and my refuge!" I pleaded with God. I simply could not believe that my son's killer had been set free.

When I looked into His Word, He was faithful to provide the answer: "With God nothing shall be impossible" (Luke 1:37 KJV). He was answering my prayer and setting me free.

"Let's pray," my husband said as he took my hand and held me close one evening. Moments like these had become our routine.

"You know," my husband began, "someday this man and our Joe might be in heaven together . . . holding hands, worshiping our Lord. We have to forgive."

Without hesitation, I agreed.

It wasn't logic, fear, or nobility that prompted us to reach this decision. It was simply a need to see beyond our circumstances and obey Jesus' commandment to forgive. We knew it was the only way we would ever heal, and we wanted more than anything to be pleasing to God. Perhaps our intense focus on God's Word and His sustaining power throughout the entire ordeal provided the grace for us to forgive.

Once this decision was made, our world changed. Our pain began to dispel with the brightness of a new day. Until I see Joe again, I'll hold my memories of him like treasures wrapped in strings of love, safely tucked away in my heart. I can focus on these memories, because the storm no longer threatens my world. Jesus took me out of that storm and pointed the way to the calm sea of peace, serenity, and renewed hope.[11]

REMEMBERING THE GOOD TIMES

by Jeanne Gibson

You'll do best by filling your minds and meditating

on . . . the best, not the worst; the beautiful, not the ugly;

things to praise, not things to curse.

PHILIPPIANS 4:8 MSG

It was our regular Tuesday afternoon writers' group, and we were listening to a fellow member as she read a bitter article about her alcoholic father. Mary's childhood experiences sounded familiar. I, too, had had an abusive alcoholic father.

My mother, two sisters, and I never knew what to expect when my father walked in the door each night. If he was sober, which happened rarely, life would follow the pattern of most of the families in our small town. But if he had stopped by a bar on his way home, we stayed as far away from him as possible.

On such nights, arguments between my parents usually got louder and louder and seldom ended without some kind of violence or threat of violence. My sisters and I would cower in our beds, desperately praying that something terrible would happen to our father so that we wouldn't have to be afraid anymore. Of course, nothing did happen to him, and the bitterness and hatred I felt increased as I grew older.

After I grew up, married, and had a family of my own, I seldom saw my father drunk, even though my mother often related tales of his latest drunken exploits. More and more, I found myself dwelling on his evil deeds.

As I listened to Mary, though, the futility of going over and over things that cannot be changed became clear to me. I found myself blinking back tears—not just for her suffering and mine—but also for the two fathers who had lived and died leaving so much bitterness and hatred behind. Was there nothing at all worthy of praise in their lives?

Nearly a week later, Philippians 4:8 came to mind. I had to read the passage several times before I realized that I had seldom given one moment to thinking on the good things about my father. Instead, I had dredged up every evil deed he had ever committed. Was it possible that any person created by a loving God could be completely evil?

In an attempt to be fair and to think on "good" things, I had to admit that there had been many bad times, but also some enjoyable ones. Why not choose, instead, to remember the good—like the year we sold cascara bark for food money because the lumber mills were on strike? Dad—a lumberjack by profession—taught us to peel and dry the bark, which he then sold to a local merchant. Dad made it seem like a great adventure. Looking back now, I think it really was.

Then there were the times Dad made hot-potato soup as an antidote for every illness. We usually felt better right away.

I also recalled the summer that Dad paid me five dollars a day to peel the trees harvested for telephone poles. During our lunch hours together, he talked to me like an adult. That fall, I enjoyed brief notoriety as the only girl in school who could use the tools of the lumberjacks' trade—a spud, a peavey, and a crosscut saw.

Then there was the day we found an orphaned deer in the woods and took it home. Dad knew a lot about animals, trees, and flowers—and generously shared his knowledge with me.

I recalled the times that Dad took my friend Geraldine and me swimming under the covered bridge and encouraged us to try diving for the first time. When Geraldine cut her foot on some broken glass, he bandaged it, carried her to the car, and drove her home.

There was the time we picked hops and the boss scolded me for having too many leaves in my sack. Dad covered for me by saying he thought it was his sack and that it wouldn't happen again.

He took me fishing once and showed me how to cast without hooking an overhead branch every time. I also remembered when he dug a grave for my pet rabbit, Muffy. He patiently waited for me to conduct an eight-year-old's version of a funeral before shoveling dirt over the shoebox that I had decorated to serve as a coffin.

It's true that it took awhile to come up with my meager list of good times with my father. I did find some—but only after I decided to look for them. If Mary hadn't shared the article about her father, then I probably would have continued to rehearse my father's sins. Instead, I am now able—most of the time—to dismiss his misdeeds. After all, they are over, done, and gone.

Occasionally another "good" memory about my father pops into my mind, and I add it to my list. It isn't always easy, though. It's easy to slip back into my old critical habits. I must often remind myself that as a Christian, my own sins have been forgiven and forgotten. Because of that, I must also be willing to forgive and forget the sins of others.

I will always be grateful to Mary for reminding me that we do have choices about what we choose to remember. Today I choose to remember only the good.

A FISHERMAN'S DAUGHTER

by Valerie J. Frost

A new heart also will I give you, and a new spirit will I put

within you: and I will take away the stony heart out of your

flesh, and I will give you an heart of flesh.

EZEKIEL 36:26 KJV

Fishing poles, tangled lines, hooks, and sinkers were staples in our house when I was a child. I learned early about fishing lures, salmon eggs, night crawlers, and other enticements that draw the fish toward the hook and into the net.

From the time I was three years old, I fished with my father in the streams of beautiful Sedona, Arizona. We kept a trailer in a tiny park, located in a secluded area called Indian Gardens, where we spent many of our weekends, holidays, and summer vacations. I looked forward to the mornings that my father would wake me hours before the sun rose. We would drive a few miles down the mountain road, park at the top of the creek bank, maneuver the descent to the water, and begin fishing downstream. We also took trips to several lakes that were within a few driving hours of our home in Phoenix. We spent many hours trolling the lake in a small silver boat. Fishing was a way of life in our family. I was a fisherman's daughter . . . and proud of it.

I confess that I practiced my fishing technique in the fishpond at our house. Two of the fish were huge golden carp, thirteen inches in length. I caught and released them several times without my parents' knowledge. How they escaped permanent damage from the hooks is a mystery. Years later, however, they did meet their demise in an unexpected manner.

Shortly before I started first grade, the tranquil moments of flowing streams and still waters were interrupted. Until then, my dad's drinking hadn't interfered with life; but at that point, his alcoholism began a quick and steady downward spiral. I don't remember much about the next few years. The memories were replaced by the disappointment and hurt caused by my father's behavior. I do recall feeling disappointed and afraid most of the time.

As the sickness progressed, his destructive anger took over our lives. It was impossible to have the neighborhood kids play at our house anymore because of the likelihood that Dad would fly into a drunken rage. Our lives were so volatile that even our trips to the beloved trailer in the mountains became nightmares. It was safer to stay home—but not much safer. There was little money for food or bills, but plenty for the alcohol that eventually destroyed my father's business, our family, and my trust.

On my eleventh Christmas, I remember expecting to meet my father at my aunt's house. When we arrived, we were told he wasn't there. I always suspected that he had hidden in the back room until we left. It's funny that I can't remember the last time I saw him, only the last time I expected to and didn't. He never contacted us again.

When I was fifteen, we moved from Phoenix to San Diego because of my stepfather's job. Losing all contact with my biological father made the move even more difficult. Later, my mother invited him to my wedding, but he didn't respond. Over the years, I made a few unsuccessful attempts to contact him, as well. His betrayal left a void that soon filled with resentment, frustration, and deep disappointment.

Over the past forty years, I have often felt that I could never forgive my father. The choices he made caused pain in the lives of many people, but God showed me that I have a choice. I can allow the Lord to empty my heart of the resentment and bitterness rooted in my past, or I can allow my past to taint the beautiful plans He has for my life in the future.

I think about the fishpond we had when I was a child and how it grew thick green algae that obscured the view of our beautiful goldfish. My stepdad decided that if he emptied, scrubbed, and painted the concrete sides and bottom of the pond with a gloss-finished paint, it would be easier to maintain. This decision taught me an important lesson. Because he used lead-based paint, the beautiful fish that we had enjoyed for years died from lead poisoning. Unless the contaminated concrete was broken up, discarded, and replaced with fresh untarnished cement, nothing would live in that pond again.

Our hearts are much like that pond. When they are "painted" with unforgiveness and bitterness, they become toxic and nothing good can live there anymore. It takes the love and forgiveness of God to break up, discard, and replace those negative feelings with the good fruit of the Holy Spirit.

Unexpectedly, God answered my prayers, and I discovered the whereabouts of my father. An unplanned visit to a Web site revealed that he had passed away in August of 1999 while living in Missouri. This information eliminated any possibility of reconciliation and left many unanswered questions.

I realize that my father made many poor choices. I know of the ones that affected me, but I have no way of knowing where he stood in his relationship to God. I could presume that he never met our Savior because if he had, he would have made an attempt to ask for my forgiveness. But Christ has shown me that it can be a long road to walk until our relationship with Him reaches a point where we have the strength to face our past. No one but God knows the condition of a man's heart. Possibly the Lord worked in my dad's life, yet he never reached the crossroads of making amends. Maybe God scraped that toxic paint from his heart so that it could be filled with the beauty of Jesus Christ.

I will never hear from my biological father again—at least on this side of heaven—and I wonder if I was the only person to pray for his salvation. I don't presume to know his relationship with God or suggest that my prayers alone may have ushered him into the kingdom. But when I look into the face of Jesus, I can rest, knowing that I did my part.

In the book of Matthew, Christ called His disciples to be fishers of men. He didn't tell us to fish for the people that we count worthy or that haven't caused pain to others or broken our hearts. Rather, Jesus admonished us to love and forgive one another. He taught us to cast the net and draw it to shore through evangelism and prayer. Christ's dying words were,

"Father, forgive them; for they know not what they do" (Luke 23:34 KJV). His example of overflowing pure love allows us to forgive as well.

God wants our hearts to be pure vessels that safely hold the people He entrusts us to pray for. If it wasn't for God's compassion, mercy, and love, we would all be like those pitiful little fish floating on that tainted pond. My heavenly Father cares enough to cleanse me and fill my heart with His desires—and not my own, so that even today I can confidently say: "I am a Fisherman's daughter . . . and I am proud of it."

GETTING BITTER OR GETTING BETTER

Dorothy's story as told to Karen Hardin

Jesus said, "Whenever you stand praying, forgive, if you have

anything against anyone; so that your Father in heaven may

also forgive you your trespasses."

MARK 11:25 NRSV

My husband, Peter, and I had three beautiful children, owned a business, and were active in church. Everything was going fine until a business reversal turned our world upside down. As a result, I went into a severe depression that eventually brought me to the brink of suicide.

I didn't want to go out or do anything. I felt betrayed by the Christian businessman whose actions had caused deep hurt, and I blamed him for our problems. Ultimately, I felt God had failed us. I began having frequent migraine headaches. Pain pills eased the pain in my head, but not in my heart. Eventually my doctor prescribed an antidepressant, as well. Knowing I needed help, but almost against my will, my husband took me to a ladies' home Bible study. Since I didn't really want to be there, I kept my pain to myself, unwilling to let them reach out and pray for me.

After weeks in this depressive state, I felt like I wanted to end my life. I waited until my children left for school and my husband had gone to the office. All I had to do was take an overdose of my prescription medication, and it would all be over. As I was going to get the pills, the phone rang. On the line was a member of our church. He had never called me before, but that day he felt compelled to call and check on me. "Dorothy, how are you?" he asked.

"Everything is just fine," I lied, crying softly, thinking about what I was planning to do. But even with a well-meaning friend, I couldn't open my heart to share my need for prayer. The conversation ended quickly; but with this diversionary call, the overwhelming thoughts of suicide had been broken. But the unforgiveness I harbored in my heart was still there.

The Bible is clear regarding the necessity of forgiveness: "Peter came to Jesus and asked, 'Lord, how many times shall I forgive my brother when he sins against me? Up to seven times?' Jesus answered, 'I tell you, not seven times, but seventy-seven times'" (Matthew 18:21). That kind of forgiveness is impossible in our own strength. Thank God He gives us His strength.

"You have to forgive," my husband, Peter, reminded me frequently.

"I have," I always responded, thinking in my heart that this was the truth. But one day as we were going up the escalator to attend church, I saw the man that I blamed for our problems. "I hope he falls and breaks his neck," I whispered to my husband. Peter gave me a knowing smile as the truth dawned in my heart. I had not really forgiven him!

While in the midst of this struggle, our pastor began teaching on the necessity of forgiveness. *That's easy for you to say,* I thought to myself. *You've never been hurt like we have.*

At that moment, I heard the Lord speak to my heart.

Dorothy, you don't understand the hurt I experienced when I hung on the cross. This time I began to ask God for what seemed impossible to me—I asked Him to help me forgive. But it wouldn't be long before my newfound resolve would be tested.

A few weeks later, as we were sitting in church, our pastor asked us to turn and shake hands with the people around us. I turned and shook the hand of a lady behind me. It was the wife of the man I had come to despise, yet somehow I never saw her face. Next I moved to shake her husband's hand. It was the moment of truth. Without a pause, I looked straight into his eyes and from the depths of my heart said to him, "God bless you."

As the words left my mouth, it was as if honey was poured over my head and down to my feet. I let go of the man's hand as I turned to Peter and whispered, "The bitterness is completely gone." When I spoke a blessing to this man, God unlocked the hurt from my heart and set me completely free.

For the past sixteen years, I have led the Bible study that my husband took me to eighteen years ago in my hour of need. During that time, almost two thousand ladies have attended, and six of the original members still participate today. The women come from all walks of life and various churches. Many were wounded by broken marriages or the betrayal of friends. Not everyone hurt in the same way, but we all faced challenges.

Because of my own painful experience, I am able to reach out to others in their time of need. I have learned that we always have a choice. We can either become bitter or become better. I would never have chosen to go through the pain we experienced, but this very pain has enabled me to help others and find my own purpose in life. I have never enjoyed life more than I do today. I love helping people and don't have time to even think of slowing down![12]

THE CARD

by Abigail Paul

Jesus said, "Come to me, all of you who are weary and carry
heavy burdens, and I will give you rest. Take my yoke upon
you. Let me teach you, because I am humble and gentle, and
you will find rest for your souls."

MATTHEW 11:28 NLT

Tears threaten as I stare at the delicate cards. Flowers, lace,
and rainbows blend together in an impossible hue of choices.
Mother's Day.

If she gets one of those cards that say nothing, she'll hate it.

I pick up the rainbow one. "Thinking of you across the
miles with a wish for a beautiful Mother's Day." Nope. She'll
be hurt by the lack of sentiment. I sigh.

A photograph of a brilliant pink rose catches my eye. "To
the one who always stood beside me . . ." Bittersweet memories
invade my day as I swallow hard. Her big eyes are full as she
tells me I'm wonderful—the most important thing in her world.
I remember the long hours she spent caring for my needs: curl-
ing my hair, shopping for me, and typing my papers.

But the scene changes. It is after a state pageant. She's
angry because I didn't win. The hour-and-a-half drive home

seems twelve hours long. In our driveway, my dad steals a minute with me. "Don't worry about it, honey. She's living vicariously through you. It was like she was the one who lost tonight."

I shake my head, hoping to erase the memories.

There has to be a card with enough praise for her and enough honesty for me.

"To the one who always understood . . ." I wish.

I had learned to lock away my deepest thoughts and think what she wanted me to think. Even now, as a grown woman, I long for her to understand.

I wish I could pick up the phone and say, "Mom, can you pray for me? I've had a rotten day." Or, "Mom, I'm scared. I'm not sure we can make it on one salary." But if I did that, she'd put on her counselor personality, feel needed, and then use it all against me later.

I blink, forcing away the picture of her on the other end of the phone.

Get on with it; the card needs to be mailed today.

The one with the butterfly is pretty. "Mom, you're always there for me." The lump in my throat is the size of a cannonball. Oh, Mom, I know you want to be.

I crave a mother who's stable enough to handle my neediness. Instead, I have a needy mother who clings to my stability. Rubbing my temples, I remember spending hours on the phone listening to her woes. My mind reaches farther back to when I was young. She would crawl into bed with me and tell me how all her problems were my dad's fault. My brother and I spent hours trying to console her, encourage her, and keep her together.

Trying to make sense of it all, I wander through the scrambled events of my childhood:

Mom and I cuddle up for an old movie with a big bowl of popcorn and long, finger-like chunks of rich cheddar cheese.

Mom starts throwing things. I flee the sound of shattering glass as her angry words are punctuated by flying dishes.

Mom and I share gentle tears as she reads *Where the Red Fern Grows.*

I panic as she threatens suicide. I tell her to put the gun away.

Mom sits with my brother and me, the big, blue Bible storybook open in her lap. We lean against her as she reads "one more," even though I can tell she's exhausted from a long day at work.

Mom runs across the railroad tracks. Dad yells at her to get in the car. She refuses, screaming that she's leaving him.

In my mind I'm a child, hiding in the bathroom to escape Mom's raging. Clinging to my favorite doll and my Bible, I pray.

The sounds of the card shop bring me back to the present as the greeting cards swim before my eyes. Even when my mom couldn't find her faith, she taught me to hang on to mine. She told me about God, and I learned to crawl up on His lap and lay my burdens there. Wiping a tear, I turn to leave, hoping a different store will have a card that works.

That day in the card shop, I didn't know that my mom had a mental illness. I had never been able to make sense of the inconsistencies in her behavior. As the year progressed, long suppressed memories began to surface in me, and I knew it was time to face my childhood and get honest with myself. I was shocked that I'd felt no emotion when horrible things had happened to me as a child. There were many things that I'd never cried about—never been angry about. A mentor helped me understand that until I admitted my real emotions, I couldn't truly forgive. I thought I had forgiven my mother; but in reality, I'd shoved down the most painful memories. I carried false guilt. I chanted, "I forgive, I forgive," without admitting the depth of the pain raging in my soul.

So as each memory came up, I owned my emotions and quit trying to excuse my mother. Now I cried. I grieved. Anger welled up as I stomped around. I called out to God and sought support from spiritual mentors. Finally, I told God every lousy emotion I felt and how my very personhood disappeared when I was around my mother—how vulnerable and scared I had been.

As I let go of the pain of each memory, I said, "But I forgive her, Lord, and I ask You to bless her."

The process gave me the courage to begin drawing boundaries. She cried and stormed, guilt-tripped, and was broken. It was all I could do to stand my ground, knowing that I would disappoint her. I struggled to relinquish the role of the perfect, dutiful daughter. Part of it was the struggle to reshape my own identity. Part of it was making choices that I knew would hurt the woman I so desperately loved. Ricocheting between grieving for her pain and grieving for my own, I faced my anger and forgave her anew. I cried out to God to help her.

Easter came. For me, the church service trumpeted no victory. The music just unlocked emotion, making me cry. I feared her mental state. I grieved her pain. I felt guilty. After the service, I couldn't talk through the sobs that erupted. Friends whisked me away from the curious stares.

"Sometimes, it's too hard to pray for someone you're close to," a friend said. "Instead of words, I just close my eyes, walk to God's throne, and give Him my loved one."

I tried it. In my mind as I prayed, I reached for my mother's hand, and we began walking toward heaven's throne. I was shocked when she jerked her hand back and glared at me. I realized I couldn't make her go to Him for help. Bewildered, I continued toward my God. He received me, and then an amazing thing happened. He left the glorious throne and went to my mom!

My breathing became quicker, lighter. The heaviness disappeared as I felt His message: *I'm not sitting here idly waiting for her to come to Me, My child. I am going after her!*

Tears of despair changed to tears of victory! It was the Easter story. God left heaven and became man to come after us. Gratitude filled me as I left my mother in God's capable hands.

Time went by. She wouldn't admit she had a problem—certainly not a mental illness. I released her again into God's hands. She fumed and hurled false accusations. I was angry, then crushed, and then I forgave, again. I took a deep breath, gave myself permission to cry and time to heal.

Mother's Day came again. I bought the first card I saw. "Mom, I'm praying for you. I love you."

WHATSOEVER THINGS ARE GOOD

by Rita Chandler

Whatsoever things are true, whatsoever things are honest,

whatsoever things are just, whatsoever things are pure,

whatsoever things are lovely, whatsoever things are of good

report; if there be any virtue, and if there be any praise,

think on these things.

PHILIPPIANS 4:8 KJV

The telephone rang, and I hurried to answer. I had no premonition of the havoc the call would wreak in my life.

"Mom, this is Sarah. I'm calling to tell you that if things do not change, I am leaving Robbie!"

Leaving her husband? Leaving my son? I could not believe what I was hearing. The two appeared to be compatible; both came from Christian families and were active in church work.

"All our troubles have been caused by you and your family!"

What is she talking about? I had no inkling that there had been any trouble. The people who knew them had predicted a very happy marriage after a wedding packed with blessings and well-wishers. Two years later when they found a house to rent, my husband and I helped clean and paint. We spent Mother's Day packing their things to move. Our youngest son installed new light fixtures and electric plugs, and made plumbing repairs. This was one of many times that our family pitched in to help, and it was our delight to do so.

The angry words spilled out in a raging torrent from the daughter-in-law who had, until then, always treated me with love and respect. My actions and attitudes, meant to show love and concern, were now interpreted as destructive. Sarah screamed, "You try to control our lives by hanging on to your son!" I felt devastated and was speechless with emotion.

Weeks passed, and the situation did not improve. Discussions with my son and his wife only brought more misunderstandings. Neither side seemed able to grasp or resolve the root issues between us. Then the letter came that ended the mother-son relationship. Robbie wrote that he had to choose between his wife and his parents, and his duty was to stay with his wife.

I could not believe this could happen to me. I spent many sleepless hours reading my Bible and praying for an answer. Special occasions, usually celebrated with the family, opened the wounds anew. I felt empty without a word from the child who, after thirty years of caring, had rejected me and our family.

I had great hopes that things might improve when my son's baby, our first grandchild, was dedicated at church and Robbie invited us to attend. My hope was shattered. He and his wife barely spoke to us. We were not invited to sit with the family or attend a celebration that followed at a restaurant. I felt betrayed by circumstances that indicated my sensitive, loving son had no regard for me or the pain I was experiencing. I longed for reconciliation and the delight of holding my darling grandchild in my arms.

In my depression and despair, I withdrew from people and activities I enjoyed, but decided to attend a banquet for mothers and daughters at our church. I went alone.

The speaker began apologetically. "I have a different message than the one I had planned," she began. "Yesterday I felt led of the Lord to change my topic and speak on a subject that seems a most unlikely message for a mother/daughter banquet."

I shifted in my chair, eager to catch every word from a speaker who had the courage to change her program when she sensed God's prompting.

"I have really wrestled with this message, because it is not one I like to speak about," she continued. "Most of us have many thoughts that we cherish, but those are not the ones I plan to address. Rather, I am going to talk about the unpleasant happenings that hurt us, the clever devices used by Satan to keep us from bearing the radiant testimony that Jesus wants for us.

"My subject focuses on the events that have left us feeling angry and bitter. The memories of those things cause us to recall each agonizing scene and conversation that demolished our joy. And if we let them, they will keep destroying us day after day."

As I listened to her words, I thought of at least two instances during the past week when I should have been joyful. Instead I remembered in detail a painful new incident caused by the break with my son and his wife.

The speaker continued, "My own mother is an example of

one who will not let go of her sorrow. She has five children. One daughter does not give her the loving attention she receives from the other four. In every conversation, she proclaims the hurt she suffers from this one. My mother chooses to dwell on her sorrow, forgetting the blessings of her other children who lavish her with attention and support."

I, too, had other children, friends, and a husband who told me of their love. Most importantly, in early childhood, I accepted Jesus as my Savior and Lord, and throughout my life, He had faithfully shown His love for me.

"Dear ladies," the speaker spoke softly, "do not let Satan rob you of your victory through Jesus Christ. No person or incident—in fact, nothing—can cause you to become angry and destroy your calm and purpose unless you let it."

I hung on every word, eager for help in my pain. As I glanced around the room, I saw that other women were listening intently, as if they, too, identified with the problem. The speaker finished her message with prayer.

I made my way through the crowd to the front of the room and clasped the speaker's hand. "Thank you, oh, thank you," I tried to speak over the lump in my throat as tears ran down my cheeks. "I know why you were asked to change your topic tonight," I said. "God knew I needed to hear your message. I feel as if He were speaking directly to me."

We had difficult years ahead, but the speaker's words continued to remind me that by changing my way of thinking, I could enjoy peace. Over and over I read the scripture in Philippians 4:8 directing me to think about the things that are true, honorable, just, lovely, and worthy of praise.

The healing of the relationship came very slowly. It

required a major letting go on my part, which I was only able to do by the grace of God. I prayed about every attempt to contact Robbie, Sarah, and my grandchild. As I felt released to do so, I sent cards and gifts for special occasions, along with notes when appropriate. Eventually, the messages were acknowledged.

One day Robbie and Sarah brought my little granddaughter to a graduation celebration for a family member that they knew we would be attending. My son placed my grandchild in my arms. I held her smooth cheeks against mine and admired the beauty of her blue eyes and perfect little body. Although my joy was mixed with pain, it was still another step in the right direction. My torment reappeared from time to time, but I was determined to focus on the positive. It was a monumental day when we were invited to my son's home once again. They have since come to ours, and we have continued in this vein for some time now.

It is unfortunate that we have not been able to truly resolve the situation with Robbie and Sarah, but God has helped me to accept it and be grateful for the time we do spend together. Who knows what the future holds; I don't concern myself with it. What I do know is that God has filled my heart with His boundless love, and it has enabled me to forgive and let go.

If God forgives us, we must forgive ourselves.

Otherwise it is almost like setting up ourselves as

a higher tribunal than him.

C. S. LEWIS

FORGIVING YOURSELF

Jesus said, "If you forgive anyone's sins,

they are forgiven. If you refuse to forgive them,

they are unforgiven."

JOHN 20:23 TLB

Are you saying that you're right and God is wrong? "What are you talking about?" you ask. "Of course not!" Okay. But let's look a little deeper into this question.

We all blow it from time to time. As believers, we know we must acknowledge our transgressions and ask God to forgive us when we sin. And we know that one of the hallmarks of Christianity is that as believers we are to forgive others when they sin against us. Much has been said and taught on these themes.

But what about forgiving yourself? Have you ever given this much thought? Sadly, if a person does not forgive himself, even though God and others may forgive him, he will remain in an emotional and spiritual prison. Forgiving others is difficult, but to forgive oneself is often an even greater challenge.

Is this the case with you? Have you committed some sin that in your eyes is unforgivable? Has what you have done caused seemingly irreversible damage? Are others suffering because of something you did or did not do?

If so, it is likely that you have struggled with forgiving yourself. Maybe you have flat refused to do so. Or maybe you think you shouldn't forgive yourself. Perhaps you can relate to those who believe that feelings of guilt and condemnation are the eternal price a person must pay for sins committed. Perhaps you can identify with those who do penance or even resort to self-punishment or self-mutilation to relieve guilt. Those behaviors will only pull you down further into desperation and despair.

In truth, there is only thing that can answer for sin and guilt, only one thing that can set people free. It is the blood of Jesus. When people complain that they can't forgive themselves, they are saying, "The blood of Jesus wasn't enough. It was enough for God to forgive me, maybe even enough for others to forgive me. But it is not enough for me to forgive myself." So ask yourself: Are you saying that you are right and that God is wrong? Are you saying that you aren't forgivable even though this contradicts what God has said in His Word? What message does that communicate to Jesus when He has already borne your punishment for you?

Consider another aspect of God's forgiveness. When He forgives you, He actually forgets your sin! "I, even I, am he who blots out your transgressions, for my own sake, and remembers your sins no more" (Isaiah 43:25). It sounds too good to be true, but He doesn't even know what you're talking about if you bring up the offense again! If He forgets it, could it be possibly be productive for you to continually rehash it?

When we refuse to forgive ourselves, we enter into one of

the devil's most insidious schemes. Satan hasn't forgotten your faults and failings, and he plans to milk them for all they're worth. He knows that as the internal pressure builds, the pot of your emotions will likely boil over and do further damage to you and others. Satan knows that if you are tangled up in self-hatred and condemnation, you won't be a threat to his destructive work in the lives of others. You will never be free to do anything except fight to keep your head above water. How can you let your light shine with dark curtains pulled over the windows of your soul? You will be forever hindered until you can release yourself. It takes the grace of God.

The Father must have known we would struggle with this, because He gave us many examples of His followers blowing it. Their dirty laundry is forever recorded in the Word of God. Take the apostle Peter. Three times he denied he even knew Jesus. This from a man who had stood with Him on the Mount of Transfiguration, witnessed His many miracles, and walked by His side for three years. But we know from the gospel accounts that Peter was exceedingly remorseful and cried bitterly. (See Matthew 26:74-75 and Luke 22:60-62.) Yet Peter not only able to receive Jesus' forgiveness, somehow he found the courage to forgive himself. Peter became one of the boldest and most effective witnesses of the New Testament.

What about the apostle Paul, the man whom God chose to write most of the New Testament? In Romans 7:22-23 TLB, he wrote: "I love to do God's will so far as my new nature is concerned; but there is something else deep within me, in my lower nature, that is at war with my mind and wins the fight and makes me a slave to the sin that is still within me. In my mind I want to be God's willing servant, but instead I find myself still enslaved to sin."

It's obvious: Paul wrestled with sin like the rest of us. We can relate to Paul as he cries out, "Oh, what a miserable person I am! Who will free me from this life that is dominated by sin?" (v. 24 NLT). But then came the revelation: "Thank God! The answer is in Jesus Christ our Lord" (v. 25 NLT).

Paul must have been able to forgive himself, because in the next chapter he gives us one of the most precious of all Bible promises: "There is therefore now no condemnation to them which are in Christ Jesus, who walk not after the flesh, but after the Spirit" (Romans 8:1 KJV). No condemnation. Imagine that coming from one who had been so radically saved, yet was still wrestling with sin!

The good news is that if you are struggling to forgive yourself, you are in good company. Indeed, there are times when it is harder to forgive yourself than it is to forgive any other person. But if you are ever to walk in true freedom and joy, you must follow the example of the apostles and forgive yourself. Let yourself go. You are the only one holding you back.

It might help to do something symbolic to settle the issue once and for all. Try this: Write your offense on a piece of paper, naming it aloud. Then place the paper in your fireplace, verbally letting go of that offense that has you bound. Finally, light the paper with a match. As you see the flame literally consuming your offense, imagine your sin being consumed as well. Then turn and walk away.

Today's your day of freedom! Rejoice and be glad!

LETTING MYSELF GO

by Sydna Massé

Jesus told the parable of the unforgiving servant,

"The king called in the man he had forgiven and said:

'You evil servant! I forgave you that tremendous debt because

you pleaded with me. Shouldn't you have mercy on your fellow

servant, just as I had mercy on you?'"

MATTHEW 18:32-33 NLT

Abortions happen in ministry families. I know, because I had one. The pressures of church life—isolation, unrealistic expectations, lack of time and communication with parents— may lead a minister's child to rebel, which can result in a crisis pregnancy. I know, because I was a pastor's daughter, and that's what happened to me. I got pregnant in 1981, when I was attending a Christian college. The father was also a PK (Preacher's Kid). We both knew the Bible condemned what we were doing, but we did it, anyway; we enjoyed the thrill of breaking the rules.

I believed I was doing everyone a favor by having an abortion. I reasoned that not only would a pregnancy get me expelled from college, it could devastate the ministries of both our families. My boyfriend insisted that abortion was the only solution, and I didn't argue. Abortion was legal, after all, and I had heard very little against the procedure. I thought I could simply erase my mistake. Yet something—or Someone—in my heart told me I would regret my decision for the rest of my life.

A few months after the abortion, I broke up with my boyfriend and transferred to a secular university. There I found a measure of comfort. The people I lived with were not Christians, and their opinions allowed me to believe that my abortion had been a good solution. I was afraid of being around Christians, thinking they would certainly condemn me if they discovered what I had done. For years I hid from God and tried to block the pain of choosing to end my baby's life.

In 1985, I graduated, and soon after, I met Tom, the man who would become my husband. As our relationship deepened, I decided to share my secret with him. He had a right to know what I'd done, and because he was a Christian, I needed to know if he could love me in spite of it. His response surprised me, and I'll never forget how loved I felt when he said, "If I had been the father, you never would have found yourself in an abortion clinic."

Tom and I married the following year, and our first son, Bruce, was born in 1988. When I held him, my conscience stirred, and the magnitude of my decision to abort my first child began to haunt me. How could I not have loved that child as much? How could I have condemned him to death? Depression, anger, sorrow, guilt, anguish, and remorse washed over me. Until then, I had held on to the false idea that I had destroyed only a blob of tissue, but Bruce's sweet face ended that fantasy.

In 1991, three months after the birth of Michael, our second son, I began working at Focus on the Family, a ministry devoted to strengthening the family. Because they are staunchly pro-life, I was haunted by the fear of being fired if anyone discovered my abortion. But in orientation class, Dr. James Dobson, the organization's founder and president, seemed to address me personally.

"I know I'm speaking to many women who have had abortions," he said. "I want you to know that there is no sin that God cannot forgive. The problem may be that you don't forgive yourself, and you may need help to do this."

He was right. I couldn't forgive myself. I didn't deserve forgiveness. After all, I had taken a small, innocent life. Tears flowed freely, and I found myself in intense grief. When a coworker told me about the post-abortion ministry at a crisis pregnancy center, I recoiled at the idea of actually addressing this pain directly, but the Lord soon convinced me that it was something He wanted me to do. That ten-week Bible study helped me confess my sin to God and grieve my child's death. At one point, I asked the Lord what had happened to my baby the day I aborted him.

He replied, *He is with me, Sydna. I have kept him safe.*

Though I had been a Christian for most of my life, only then did I feel I could finally come home, and the warmth of the welcome was incredible. As I opened my heart to the Lord, I rediscovered the joy of having the Holy Spirit in my life.

But as good as it felt to be forgiven by God, I still struggled to forgive myself. Then one day I was led to read the parable of the unforgiving servant in Matthew 18. God had forgiven my sin just like the King who pardoned the great debt. But then I saw that He expected me to do the same with others—including myself. I had to forgive my old self. As I acted on this revelation and obeyed what I felt the Lord was leading me to do, I was finally able to let go of the unforgiveness I had held toward myself.

Yes, there are times when the accuser of the brethren (See Revelation 12:10.) reminds me of my past transgression, but it no longer has the power over me that it once did. As I behold the face of my Redeemer, I remind myself that I am forgiven; and like He does, I choose to remember my sin no more.[13]

RECOVERING FROM MY MORTAL SIN

by Ed Gungor

I know my transgressions, and my sin is always before me.

Cleanse me with hyssop, and I will be clean; wash me, and I

will be whiter than snow.

PSALM 51:3,7

I had an affair. And it was disastrous. I wish I could say it happened because I had a bad marriage. It didn't. In fact, Gail and I had a wonderful one. I was the senior pastor of a church that grew from zero to 4,500 in just under three years. I had more career success and opportunity than I knew what to do with. But as I climbed the ladder of success, I began to lose my inner spiritual tone and discovered that the ladder I was climbing was leaning against the wrong wall—one that did not satisfy. Not only had my work become empty, I entered what I now understand to be a full-blown midlife crisis.

Dr. James Dobson defines *midlife crisis* as "a time of intense personal evaluation when frightening and disturbing thoughts surge through the mind, posing questions about who I am and why I'm here and what it all matters. It is a period of self-doubt and disenchantment with everything familiar and stable. . . . These anxieties," Dobson continues, "often produce an uncomfortable separation between loved ones at a time when support and understanding are desperately needed."[14]

Without realizing I was acting in a textbook fashion, I found myself distancing myself from my safe relationships and from my wife of more than twenty years. Dobson captures the danger of an unchecked midlife crisis: "At this delicate point in a man's life, Satan reaches into his ugly bag of tricks and retrieves the most foul of all his suggestions: adultery. . . . When [the] fling has run its course, [the participants] must face the spouses they have betrayed and the children they have abandoned and the God they have disobeyed. The consequences of their sin will reverberate through eternity, hurting the innocent as certainly as the guilty."[15]

Infidelity can shatter a marriage. It's one of the top reasons given for divorce, a result that even has biblical justification. But when I came to Gail with my sin, she chose to hold on to our marriage instead of throwing me out. That took uncommon courage and great grace. Unless a person has walked through this type of tragedy, it's difficult to understand its magnitude. Psychologists have said that on an emotional level, a woman would prefer to be raped by a gang of men than see her husband involved with another woman. But Gail—looking past the pain of her betrayal—believed our marriage mattered. She believed that forgiveness and grace were bigger than failure. Her daring love provided the fodder I needed to begin my long journey back to normalcy.

For the majority of my life, I had maintained a tender heart before God. My sins had mostly been internal and attitudinal. Whenever I blew it, I went to God to receive forgiveness. But receiving forgiveness and getting up spiritually after falling into adultery proved to be almost insurmountable. By the time my sin came to light, it had taken a terrible toll. I was little more than a shadow of what I had once been. It took me awhile to really buy into the fact that God's forgiveness is limitless. It took me awhile to push past my sense of guilt and shame, and trust that God had indeed sent away my sin "as far as the east is from the west" (Psalm 103:12).

From the moment I began tumbling into moral disaster to the many months after it ended, deep waves of shame and hopelessness ravaged me. When I was younger, I used to pray, "God, I would rather die prematurely than act in a way that would bring dishonor to You." Yet not only did I dishonor God, I shamed the wife of my youth and our four precious children (in their teen and adult years). I embarrassed and shamed my friends, my colleagues, my staff, and the tens of thousands of people I had ministered to over my twenty-plus years of public ministry.

As I entered my sin, it was like belly-flopping into a lake from five hundred feet in the air—I lay motionless with all the spiritual wind knocked out of me. Physically, I felt like I was going to die. Emotionally, I was numb. I couldn't sleep. I grew depressed and withdrawn. Everything I had stood for had been torn out of me in a moment—and I didn't have the courage to repent or ask for help.

This torment went on for months. I kept thinking, *I can figure this out.* But there are some things that we cannot figure out by ourselves—in fact, in my situation, freedom didn't come until I confessed my sin to others and asked them to pray for me. (See James 5:16.) The longer I stayed in the sin and kept it from others, the more it destroyed me. As I panicked to cover my tracks, I chose to toss away my integrity. It seemed much easier to destroy my soul than it was to build it up. And on some level, part of me felt like I deserved to be destroyed. I had ignored the warning given by Job: "I made a covenant with my eyes not to look lustfully at a girl" (Job 31:1). Consequently, I reaped the predicted devastation: "Adultery is a fire that burns the house down; I wouldn't expect anything I count dear to survive it" (Job 31:12 MSG).

I live in Oklahoma, and we know the destruction wrought by tornados. We have seen the look in the eyes of a family standing on the site of what was once their home. No words can describe the paralyzing loss they experience. No one in their right mind would wish this kind of disaster on even their worst enemy; yet like a tornado, I destroyed my life and the lives of many close to me. To this day, some of those people are still struggling to recover.

Years have passed now. Not only have Gail and I survived—we have begun to thrive. We are lovers and best friends again. We know the ache and pain of sin, but we know what it is like to experience God's restoration. My family and a number of close friends (and a great professional counselor) stood by us, trusting God's mercy to help us replant what I had uprooted.

Understandably, some will never forgive me, but I am finally at the place where I can leave that in God's hands. I can never undo what I did, but I continue to trust God to heal and restore those injured by my sin. It is difficult to smile at life when I think of the result of my failure; but as I open the pages of Scripture, I find hope. Wonderful leaders like Moses and David fell into serious sin; and while there were consequences,

God still salvaged their lives and His dreams for them. The pages of Scripture shout that there is hope beyond failure.

There are two central keys that have helped Gail and me navigate the course back to wholeness. The first is forgiveness. My favorite definition of the word *forgiveness* as used in the New Testament could be translated "to hurl (e.g., missiles)."[16] In the Old Testament, Micah 7:19 says that God will "hurl all our iniquities into the depths of the sea." When we apply the blood of Jesus to a sin we have committed, it causes that sin to be hurled from us like a missile blasting away forever! What a picture this has painted for me. When God forgives us, He doesn't even remember our sin! (See Isaiah 43:25.)

Still, it takes a continuous, daily gesture of faith to see a major failure like this one being hurled into God's sea of forgetfulness. Every time I run into evidence of my failure—from a distrustful look of a past parishioner to the memory of a lost lifelong friendship—I grieve deeply. These artifacts of my failure scream, "Look at what you did!" At that point, I have a choice. I can either take God at His Word and "millimeter" my way back to wholeness, or I can spin out into more death. Death stinks. So I practice forgiveness. I practice accepting it from God; I extend it toward those who reject, condemn, and mistreat me; and I practice forgiving myself. (See Matthew 6:12.)

The second key has been patience. Years ago I worked in a physical-therapy department. My work with those with minor problems was short-lived. I would help them do the exercises for awhile and then show them how to continue the work at home.

With patients who had had serious accidents or major

surgeries, the process was much slower. The key was to go only as fast as the person could handle without losing ground. I remember one patient who had been in a bad car accident and was bedridden for six months. Our first full week in therapy was spent just helping him sit up at a ninety-degree angle on the pivoting bed. He cried and agonized over the millimeters of progress he made.

Sometimes it takes awhile for us to get right. The more serious the sin, the longer the recovery. For a long time, my progress could only be measured in millimeters. It seemed that no matter how hard I tried to recapture the strength I had always known in my soul, the more it eluded me. It was like I had spiritual amnesia—I could remember glimpses of what it was like to love God and to be right, but grasping and securing those things was like trying to snatch a bolt of lightning. It wasn't until I stopped trying to control the whole thing and just stayed honest and open to the input and help of others that spiritual health began to return. The fact was that I had been mortally wounded—and accepting that fact helped to speed up my recovery.

Hopefully, others will never experience a tragedy like ours (and I do believe that kind of tragedy can be prevented). But for those who have fallen, as well as for those who have been hurt, the good news is that God wants to help—to "join" us. Gail and I found that He offered strength to help us overcome what should have destroyed us. He gave us grace to forgive what should have divided us. He gave us courage to work through what needed to be honestly faced; and He gave us hope in seasons when despair tried to get the upper hand.

During those darkest days, in surprising ways, God was

working even when we didn't think He was. I have come to believe that no matter what, God is always lovingly nudging us toward the help we need—even when we don't seem to be aware of it. Occasionally I lift my head and it is as if I see Him smiling and nodding approvingly at me. I believe if we will do our best to stay open to Him (even if our efforts seem vain), He will always lead us back to wholeness by giving us His forgiveness and helping us forgive ourselves. No matter what we have been through, there is always hope in God.

FROM MUNDANE TO MIRACULOUS!

by Sonja Brown

Our soul has escaped as a bird out of the snare of the trapper;

the snare is broken and we have escaped.

PSALM 124:7 NASB

It started like any other road trip home. I awoke before sunrise, coaxed my sleepy mind to go through its proverbial checklist to see if I had forgotten anything, and then made my way to my car. I took a moment to still my heart before I pulled out of the drive, asking God for protection and that the Holy Spirit would go before me to make this an uncommon time of connecting with my family.

Trips home had not always been the most enjoyable for me. Our family was sort of a "mini-series" family—always so much drama. Invariably, somewhere during the four- to five-day visit, a conversation would begin that kept the memories of our generational abnormalities in the very front and center. I hoped this would not be another holiday defined by the past rather than focusing on the future.

The past—that was the culprit. Old memories . . . old mindsets . . . old reactions. Why couldn't we just put a nail in the coffin of our family dysfunctions? What was it about "old dialogue" that created such a slow burn of aggravation and discomfort in my soul? I was about to come face to face with the realization that my environment wasn't the problem—it was my attempt to distance myself from anyone or anything that accentuated my wounds of guilt and shame. Over the years, I had kept myself anchored behind a facade of bustling activity, while my heart was growing dull and very crowded. Through this vulnerable season, I had deeply compromised some of my core values of purity, faithfulness, and honesty. I found it difficult, at best, to truly and completely forgive myself. This was no longer a case of a fleeting thought of unworthiness. My unforgiveness had escalated into a full-blown demonic assignment over my life, a low-lying black cloud of condemnation that shadowed me persistently.

I always had plenty of time to muse over these issues during the ten-hour drive from Oklahoma to Tennessee; however, I had no idea that this time I was headed for a glorious God-intrusion—one that would confront my skewed perceptions and damaged emotions. I was getting ready to make a quantum leap from the mundane to the miraculous!

About five hours into my journey, I was listening to a message by Joyce Meyer called "Beauty to Ashes." At a significant moment, 2 Corinthians 5:19 NASB resonated deep in my spirit: "That God was in Christ reconciling [us] to himself, not counting [our] trespasses against [us]." In a split second, a tsunami of revelation crashed upon my heart! God was in Christ, not holding my trespasses against me! Translation? A shining key had just unbolted the rusty door of my prison cell. I walked out of spiritual detainment empowered to forgive myself and be released from the stronghold of an afflicted and storm-tossed heart.

The Holy Spirit swept over my soul, and it was as if God had jolted me from a deep sleep. All of a sudden, the sheer force of God's love was shed abroad in my heart, and I walked into the fiery furnace of mercy. *I was forgiven!* Through God's extravagant presence, I was transported from trauma to transparency!

I hadn't realized how buried my insecurities had become and how masterfully the residue of past mistakes had been concealed. It took honest prayer and a sovereign act of transcendent grace to dismantle the house of lies that had kept me repressed and living in a cave of fear and regret.

Most people do not feel comfortable unearthing and disclosing their shortcomings, because they fear being judged, misunderstood, or rejected. The layers of self-imposed unforgiveness can lodge deeply, and it takes a supernatural, God-powered revelation to set a captive heart free. It was time to begin the process of forgiving myself. One of the greatest lessons I've learned is to be quick to believe that Jesus understood the depth of extreme forgiveness when He drank the bitter cup of all my mistakes and failures. He was "numbered with the transgressors" (Isaiah 53:12 NASB)—He identified with me, invested redemption in me, and reaped the harvest of my freedom!

So there I was—catapulted into this radical celebration, right there in my car. Was I speeding? Was I even on my side of the road? I could hardly see anything through the floodgate of tears. I found myself "gushing" what my heart wanted to express—extreme thankfulness, exceeding praise to the Shepherd of my soul!

As I reveled in this newly found dimension of forgiveness,

God showed me that in order to become fully alive, I had to let down my pretenses and let go of others' opinions and perceptions of me. Instead, I had to fix my gaze on God's heroic, irrational, extravagant love. His love redeems and restores. His love enabled me to forgive myself!

As the salty tears continued to stream down my face, I was now hundreds of miles closer to my destination. My prayer had availed: "Holy Spirit, make this an uncommon time of life, love, and laughter with my family!" As I pulled into the driveway of my sister's home, I knew that the stone of resistance had been rolled away. Perfect love had done its perfect work—casting out every trace of fear, hesitation, and doubt.

Bags in hand, I gently shouldered open the large red door. When I crossed the threshold and reached out to my family, I felt as if the arms of God had come from behind and wrapped around us. I felt secure, comforted, and undergirded. The Red Sea had parted, and I walked across on dry ground. The compelling, tangible love of Jesus walked into that house. People sense forgiveness and freedom and want to be close to it—and that's how the next few days unfolded. Our family stuck close, laughed hard, and created new memories.

The Lord has been passionate about restoring my sense of beauty before Him and turning my mourning into dancing. By forgiving myself, I have chosen sanctuary over sorrow and healing over heartache. I have learned that there is no mistake or failure that is beyond His infinite grasp. I'm forgiven by the One who loves and enjoys me the best. And He alone is the ultimate reason I have for forgiving myself. I'm forgiven and now I have a reason for living—really living!

A JOURNEY OF THE HEART

by Kim Ford

We know that all that happens to us is working for our good if

we love God and are fitting into his plans.

ROMANS 8:28 TLB

At four years old, I noticed the difference. Steve's legs didn't work like mine. He had cerebral palsy.

Steve spent his days at physical therapy, where therapists tried desperately to get his legs to function properly. For two years, my mom faithfully made the five-hundred-mile trip each week, with three small children in tow. It was only way she could give my brother an opportunity to live as normal a life as possible.

Sadly, after years of therapy, Steve was still confined to a wheelchair. His body continued to grow, but his ability to function became more difficult as his crippled legs refused to respond.

I remember as a child going out to play and then running back to check on Steve. That is when I remember my first twinge of guilt. Why did I have two legs that did what I wanted them to do, when Steve had no control over his? I could run and jump, but Steve couldn't even stand. I felt guilty for all the things I could do that Stephen couldn't. Even as a seven year old, I knew it wasn't fair for me to have so much while my brother had so little.

As Stephen grew, so did his physical needs. This adult-sized teenager not only had to be lifted in and out of the bed and the bathtub, but my mom also had to carry him to and from the car and everywhere we went. Even running the smallest errand became a monumental task.

During this time, my mother had surgery, making it impossible for her to carry Steve. My parents finally made the tough decision to put him into a home for the handicapped. Although Steve loved his new home, he greatly missed us. We missed him, too, and visited him often. Yet each time we had to go home and leave him behind, sadness and grief would sit on me like huge weights, threatening to press the life out of me. Although I hate to admit it, I imagined what it would have been like to have a "normal" big brother. Why did it have to be this way?

I carried this guilt into adulthood. I didn't feel like I could ever do enough for my brother. He was no longer the cute little boy crawling on the floor; he was now a grown man, restrained by a body that did not allow him to live and function like others. My life was so normal and his so abnormal. Somehow, I reasoned, it must be my fault.

After graduating from high school, I left home to attend a Christian university where I became the chaplain on my dormitory floor. One day I was talking with the women's chaplain that I served under. Wanting to get to know me, Mary asked questions about my family. In the course of the conversation, I told her about Steve and his condition. Then, to my amazement, she exclaimed, "Kim, now I understand why you're such a special person. It must be because of Steve."

"What?" I asked. "What do you mean? I feel so guilty when I think about him. I have so much, and he has so little. I've spent my whole life looking over my shoulder, feeling badly about leaving Steve behind. It makes me sad that he has been so restricted; and when anything good happens in my life, I feel undeserving."

My wise friend shared further. "God certainly did not cause Steve's affliction, but He can take any situation—no matter how difficult—and cause good to come from it. That's what I believe has happened in your life. You are sensitive to others. You take the time to connect with people. You truly care about those around you. People aren't just born that way, Kim. As a child, you helped Steve and were often his legs. You were forced to think and care for others because of your brother's unusual needs. It seems to me that Steve is one of the greatest gifts you've ever been given. The tenderness and sensitivity I see in you is because of him."

That day, I began to look at my life with new eyes. I began to see Steve differently as well. Although I had always been grateful for being "healthy," I had not fully recognized and appreciated the gift my brother had been in my life. I was able to forgive myself for that, and I was able to let go of the guilt I had carried. My eyes began to open to all that I had learned because of Steve. That day I began to understand myself better. I left Mary a changed person.

As I understood myself better, I was free to love Steve more fully. He has since passed away, but not before I had a better understanding of all the things he brought to my life. As God cleansed my heart of heaviness, I felt a sincere gratitude for the love and mercy God developed in me through my relationship with Steve. I understood so little growing up with a handicapped brother, yet God has so tenderly crafted me to be exactly what He wants and needs me to be.

Steve may have lived his life without the use of his legs, but what he gave me has taken me to places that I never could have walked alone.

THE CHILD WITHIN

by Craig Nelson

Jesus said, "'Love your neighbor as you love yourself.'"

MATTHEW 19:19 NCV

You know those miserable images of being the last one chosen when asked to "team up" for a game in elementary school? Those images were reality for me. I weighed nearly twice what others my age weighed, so being chosen last was only the beginning of my problems. My weight made me the target of jokes and constant humiliation. As a result, I learned to be self-abusive and made fun of myself before anyone else had a chance.

As I grew older and lost weight, I didn't lose my talent at quick wit and self-directed put-downs. I became more critical of myself than ever. Lying in bed at night, I would think about the stupid things I had done and said during the day, and I would verbally kick myself to sleep. Little did I know that I was becoming my own worst enemy.

While in my early twenties, during a period of intense prayer, I saw the image of a young boy—he looked to be about twelve years old—in my mind's eye. The boy was sitting in a corner, crying, with his arms wrapped around himself. I sensed he was frightened, alone, and suffering from some great hurt.

I felt that God wanted me to pray for this boy so that He could touch him and take away his pain and anguish. My heart went out to him. As I prayed, I asked God to show me who the boy was and what was causing him such torment.

To my amazement, God showed me that I was that young boy. I knew that I needed to apologize to that boy for the way I had treated him all his life. I had ridiculed him, put him down, and treated him as though he were totally worthless. It was time for me to start treating myself with love, the same love that Jesus had shown me. I was overwhelmed. Tears flowed uncontrollably. Then, when I asked that little boy for forgiveness, I sensed a thorough healing taking place deep inside me. I learned that by allowing God to give me the love I needed to love myself, I could, in turn, love others more fully.

TRANSFORMED BY THE TRUTH

by Paula Moldenhauer

Let God transform you into a new person

by changing the way you think.

ROMANS 12:2 NLT

I grabbed the plastic container of leftover peas and flung it across the kitchen floor, my anger rising as the lid popped off and the green beads cascaded over the linoleum like a chartreuse hailstorm. As my son watched, I began to cry. I never wanted him to see behavior like that. I never wanted to lose control. I wanted him to have a perfect home, the stability that I had longed for as a child.

"What's wrong, Mommy?" he squatted next to me as I cleaned up, wiping tears as I worked.

"I'm just so sorry I lost my temper, sweetheart. I never want to do things that make Jesus sad."

My pragmatic little man shrugged his shoulders and cocked his head. "Just ask Jesus to forgive you. He will."

I nodded. Of course—Jesus forgives. I'd known that all my life. But I didn't feel better. I couldn't forgive myself.

I spent the next few years working very hard to be good— and I would be, for a while. But it always happened. I'd have a few sleepless nights, some financial stress, or the kids would fuss and I'd say something unkind or lose my temper. Then my guilt would return, stronger than ever. I'd wallow in my inability to be the perfect mother, feel unworthy, hate myself—and a couple of times, when no one was around to see it, I slapped myself. I wanted to hurt myself for hurting others. Sometimes the guilt would linger for days, clouding my ability to be the very person I longed to be. It kept me in a cycle of perfectionism, failure, guilt, and condemnation. And I wondered why God sometimes seemed so far away.

After a confrontation with a loved one, I took a realistic look at myself and made an appointment to meet with a freedom ministry at my church.[17] Painful memories I'd shoved inside assaulted me. Over the course of two days, we spent seventeen hours together, praying through issues of fear, perfectionism, and unforgiveness in my life. I came to understand that I'd taken on a whole suitcase full of false identities and carried them with me. No wonder I struggled with self-hatred. I also realized that sometimes I wasn't really mad at myself. Sometimes the anger that spilled out was toward other people, but I took the blame upon myself. The facilitators walked me through the hard task of forgiving others and then helped me forgive myself.

At the end of the session, they handed me a list of truths based on Scripture and asked me to read through them. They said I needed to replace the lies in my life with God's truth. I began reading in a steady tone, but soon my voice broke and I cried as I read, "I am free forever from condemnation (Romans 8:1-2) . . . I am free from any condemning charges against me (Romans 8:31-34) . . . I cannot be separated from the love of God (Romans 8:35-39) . . . I am confident that the good work

God has begun in me will be perfected (Philippians 1:6) . . ."[18]
When I finished, I looked at the facilitators in wonder. All
that guilt, all that condemnation, and all the fear that I would
never be good enough didn't stand up to the truth in God's
Word. I was totally forgiven, and God wanted me to forgive
myself. He didn't want me living in constant shame, beaten
down by the mountains of my inadequacies.

My freedom session took place several years ago. Since
then, I've been rebuilding my life on the truth of God's Word.
God is showing me that no one is perfect but Him and that
instead of working so hard to be good—and to never mess
up—I need to focus on the height, depth, and breadth of His
love (Ephesians 3:16-19). God is showing me that He never
turns away from me when I fail. Instead of looking away in
shame, God wants me to run to Him. I am always accepted, no
matter what I've done, and He wants me to accept myself the
way He does—just as I am.

About two years after my freedom session, I totally blew it.
I lost my temper and said something awful to my daughter.
When I saw the pain in her eyes, I couldn't stand it. I took a
drive to cool down, self-hatred washing over me again. I wanted to punish myself for hurting my precious angel, and I
slapped my face. Then I made a fist and slugged my jaw.
Shocked, I sobbed harder. I'd never hit myself with a fist
before, but I did it again. "Oh, God! Help!" I cried out.

The cell phone rang. My children wanted me to come back
home. I tried to calm myself as I pulled into my driveway,
walked into my house, and knelt before my daughter. I offered
my sincere apologies. I struggled to stop crying and went to my
bed to just lay there. My son came in and said, "Mom, I think

God wants me to read this to you." I don't remember which Bible verse he shared—only that it helped. My daughter walked in and snuggled up to me. "Mom, I forgive you."

Before long all four children piled on the bed with me. "We put our money together so you don't have to cook," they explained. "We even have a coupon. Can we order pizza?"

I ruffled my little boys' hair and held them all close, reveling in the sweetness of their forgiveness. And I forgave myself. We ordered the pizza and cuddled together for the afternoon, getting lost in a good book.

As I look back on that experience, I'm awed that I could act that badly without it turning into an all-day catastrophe. Before, when I felt that I had to be perfect and couldn't forgive myself, I would have wallowed for days lost in the fog of guilt. I felt a little raw the rest of the week, but I also felt the joy of victory. I had chosen not to linger in self-hatred.

Now, I am beginning to understand that forgiveness is always mine and that the Father wants me to let go of my failures. I don't have to hurt myself; Christ took my punishment upon the cross. When I hear whispers of condemnation, it's really the enemy of my soul trying to steal my joy, tear me out of my Father's arms, and destroy me. But as I live in forgiveness, the old anger doesn't come as often or as severely—and when it does come, I'm learning how to handle it.

The first year after my freedom session, I repeated Romans 8:1 many times to myself. When those unforgiving, guilty thoughts would blast over me like an icy wind, I'd pray out loud, "There is therefore now no condemnation for those who are in Christ Jesus" (Romans 8:1 NASB). When condemning thoughts would sneak into my mind like a slithering snake, I'd whisper the verse again. As I clung to this scripture, I replaced the lie that I couldn't forgive myself, with the truth that I was already forgiven.

I know I'll continue to fail. My flesh is human. But because Jesus is in my heart, there is a spirit living inside me that is good, loving, and perfect. All that other stuff is just my flesh acting up. I'm learning not to despair when I blow it, but to fix my eyes on Jesus who is the author and perfecter of my faith (Hebrews 12:2). And I trust that He who began a good work in me will be faithful to complete it (Philippians 1:6). I run to my Father when I mess up and let Him wrap His arms around me. I'm learning to take a deep breath, say "I'm sorry," and forgive myself.

CRY OUT TO HIM!

by Georgia Paul

O LORD my God, I cried out to You, and You healed me.

O LORD, You brought my soul up from the grave;

You have kept me alive, that I should not go down to the pit.

PSALM 30:2-3 NKJV

Several years ago, I went through a very difficult time in my life—and it was my fault. During my sophomore year of college, I was juggling the responsibilities of being a dormitory leader, working a part-time on-campus job, and taking a full eighteen hours of classes. My only free time seemed to be between 1 A.M. and 7 A.M. I knew that people were counting on me to be faithful on my job; others were expecting me to fulfill the requirements for my dormitory role. So . . . I relaxed a bit in one of my classes—and ended up failing it! It was a gym class, of all things, a requirement every semester for every student at this private university.

Fortunately, during the spring semester, I was able to retake the course, in addition to being enrolled in the required gym course for that semester. I also added summer-missions training to my schedule and soon found that my ability to manage all these things was not a skill I had yet perfected. I ended up failing the repeat gym course and a Bible course. I also got a D in one of my major courses, which ironically happened to be in physical education. All of this, and I was preparing to be a teacher! I wondered what kind of teacher I would be if I kept failing courses.

The second failure in the first gym course meant that I was placed on academic probation at the university. Faced with the danger of being kicked out of school, I had to review some serious implications. If I were asked to leave, I would probably be able to complete my degree at another school. But there was an additional problem. The laws affecting teacher certification had recently changed. I currently fell under the old requirements that were being grandfathered out. At a new school, I would have to enter under the new requirements, which would take five years to complete.

I knew that being kicked out of the university might mean that I would never become a teacher. As if that weren't bad enough, many of my family members were involved with this university. All four of my grandparents worked there. My grandfathers had each helped set up different departments when the university was first established. All of my aunts and uncles had attended this university, and it is where my parents met. I winced as I considered the possibility of bringing shame to them.

The guilt was overwhelming. I was sure it would be impossible to forgive myself if I disappointed my family. And I knew that if I did not make a change, the dreams I had had for my life would not come to pass. This setback initiated the anticipation of failure. Even though I had known the Lord as my Savior for many years and had been walking with Him, I found myself in a pit of anxiety of my own making.

The circumstances would not change. I had to change myself, and I didn't know how to do it. So instead, I just gave up. I found myself sitting in an empty room with my back to the wall and my knees pulled up to my chest, crying.

It was there that God came to my rescue. My troubled mind settled on a terrifying image. I was lying on a stone slab, dead in a dark tomb. But before I could panic, the Lord showed me that this image represented me trying to live my life in my own strength.

It was true. The best I could do on my own was fail. If anything good was going to come of my life, then it would have to be because of Him. I asked God to resurrect my life, and I told Him that from then on I was going to live my life for Him and do whatever He wanted me to do. Then the mental picture changed, and I saw myself sit up!

I could relate to the psalmist: "I asked the LORD for help, and he answered me. He saved me from all that I feared. . . . The LORD hears good people when they cry out to him, and he saves them from all their troubles" (Psalm 34:4,17 NCV). I cried out to Him, and He delivered me from that terrible pit.

I looked honestly at myself and realized that I had made mistakes. I acknowledged that they were things I could have prevented and should have avoided. But I knew that if I did not decide to forgive myself and accept God's forgiveness, then my life would be a shadow filled with regret about what could have been. I chose to accept His love and forgiveness for my failures and continue walking the path He had for me.

It was not easy to do. Every time I saw my family, they asked me if I had been fulfilling my exercise requirement and completing my class assignments. It was a constant reminder of my failure. But I held on to the promises in God's Word and focused on His acceptance of me whenever I got discouraged. Also, many times that image of me sitting up on the stone encouraged me to press on in my pursuit of excellence because the Lord had given me another chance.

Fortunately, my situation did not turn out to be the catastrophe that it easily could have. God turned it around! I took a summer correspondence course for the Bible class I had failed, as well as a summer gym class, and made an A in both. The next semester, I retook the education class and passed it also. Not only did I finish on time, but I also graduated cum laude. But God wasn't through with me yet. He enabled me to go on to earn a master's degree from the same university, and I was humbled to receive an award for being the top student in my major!

Today, I am living the dream that I once feared was slipping through my fingers. In fact, God has expanded my vision, and I am doing even more! As I have been faithful in my promise to live for Him, He has enabled me to travel to South Africa, Los Angeles, Panama, Mexico, and Russia on eleven mission trips. I am in my fifth year of teaching elementary students, and I love it. God has "turned my mourning into joyful dancing. [He has] taken away my clothes of mourning and clothed me with joy" (Psalm 30:11 NLT)—and He began the moment I cried out to Him!

A BEAUTIFUL DREAM

by Renie Szilak Burghardt

I will turn their mourning into joy,

and will comfort them, and give them joy for their sorrow.

JEREMIAH 31:13 NASB

I never knew my real mother. She died in Hungary just a
few weeks after my birth. She was only nineteen years old. And
I hardly knew my father. He was the young man who came to
visit me occasionally at my grandparents' house.

I lived with my maternal grandparents since my young father
was a soldier serving in World War II. I hardly ever saw him; and
when I did, I felt shy and uncomfortable in his presence. He was
like a stranger to me. But in the summer of 1943, when I was
almost seven, he came to visit me and brought me a red bicycle
as a gift. I remember my father teaching me to ride that bicycle;
and later that day, we went for a ride out of the village and ended
up at the marsh, near the river. It was the place where the white
storks went to feed, and as we stood and watched, several of
them were foraging with their long, red beaks. I was enchanted.

"Your mother loved this marsh," my father told me gently.
"And this is where I first met her."

"Really?" I looked at him shyly. Hardly anyone ever spoke
to me about my mother.

"Yes, we met when your mama was only fourteen and I was fifteen. I came to the marsh and saw this beautiful young girl with a paper and pencil, engrossed in trying to draw the storks. When she finally noticed me, she smiled and stole my heart. We were married four years later."

Moved by his memory, I remember shyly taking his hand. We rode back together in silence; and before he left, my father promised that one day, after the war was over, we would get to know each other better. I felt strangely sad as I watched him leave. My father never got to keep his promise. It was the last time I ever saw him.

We lost track of my father over the next four years as we traveled across Hungary, looking for a safe refuge from the war. And when the war ended, Soviet occupation brought more fear and hardship. My grandparents and I escaped our war-torn country in 1947, landing in a refugee camp in neighboring Austria. We had only the clothes on our backs and no way of knowing where my father was or if he had even survived the war.

In 1951, we were blessed when we were cleared to immigrate to the United States of America. A new life in a wonderful new country lay ahead. We were grateful to God. As the ship carrying us to America moved out to sea, I thought about my father and the promise he had made the last time I saw him.

In America, my grandparents went to work, and I went to school. Life was busy and good, and the memories of my father faded. Then one night, I had a dream. My mother was asking me to find him.

To my surprise, I was able to locate my father. We wrote letters and talked on the phone. He seemed happy that I was in America, "the land where everything is possible," he told me.

I did not go to Yugoslavia, where he lived, to visit with

him, even though I knew how much he wanted to see me. Instead I married and was soon raising a family. Life was busy. But I sent him pictures of his grandchildren and told him about my life. As the years passed, my children left home, and my marriage fell apart—but I still did not go to see my father.

Then in early 1987, I received a letter from my father that broke my heart.

"Dear Daughter, I am very ill. I have lung cancer and am dying. Please bring me some good medicine from America to help me get well. And if you come and see me, that will be the best medicine of all," part of the letter read, and it was written in very shaky handwriting.

I called to tell him that there wasn't any "good medicine"—even in America—that would cure him, but that I would and come and see him just as soon as I could make the arrangements. But when I called, a relative informed me that my father had been buried earlier that day. I was too late!

I prayed that night, and with teary eyes asked God to forgive me for not granting my father's wish long ago. I fell asleep late; my eyes were swollen from all the crying. My heart ached for the man who had brought me a red bicycle when I was seven and told me how he had met my mother. I cried to think that I hadn't made more of an effort to see him before it was too late.

For days, guilt and sadness enveloped me. I could barely function. Finally, I turned to God and asked Him to bring me some closure, comfort, and relief from the terrible guilt.

Then I had a beautiful dream. I saw my father and mother, young and beautiful, walking together by the marsh, holding hands, and smiling at each other. My heart was consoled, and I could forgive myself. And I had the distinct feeling that my father had forgiven me, as well.

REMORSE AND RECOMPENSE

by Sue Foster

My iniquities have gone over my head;

they weigh like a burden too heavy for me.

I confess my iniquity, I am sorry for my sin.

PSALM 38:4,18 RSV

"Lord, what was I thinking? I wouldn't have even contemplated it had I known how much guilt and shame I would suffer over the years." Tears welled up in my eyes as I once again relived the incident from a dozen years ago.

My two young daughters owned a Brio train set at the time. They enjoyed designing various track configurations with the wooden pieces—straight and curved, two- and three-way track pieces, bridges, and tunnels. Painted in primary colors, the railroad cars coupled together magnetically. Once assembled, the girls delighted in navigating the train along the circuitous route. Truth be told, my husband and I had as much fun playing with the train set as our daughters did.

One day I visited a toy store, intent on purchasing a three-way track piece to augment their collection. Examining the price tag, I exclaimed, "Sixteen dollars for a piece of wood!" Then I covertly transferred that track piece into the box belonging to a two-way piece and vice versa. Approaching the checkout counter, I rationalized, *I'm still paying for the track, so it's not really shoplifting.* I paid the cashier and drove home, conscience clear. Not until the renewing of my Christian faith several years later did I begin to experience pangs of guilt.

Now wiping away tears, I prayed, "Father, I know that I repented and received forgiveness from You years ago. Why can't I let it go and forgive myself?" Deep inside I knew the answer. I needed to make restitution. Chills shot down my spine, and my heartbeat quickened at the thought. "Oh, Lord! Please don't make me do that! It's much too humiliating!"

Sometime later, tuning in to the Guidelines Christian radio broadcast, I listened to the host, Dr. Harold Sala, relate the testimony of a well-known Korean pastor. This individual had flown to the United States at seventeen years of age, paying child's fare. Feeling remorse, he endeavored to reimburse the airline for the adult/child ticket price differential nine years later. The airline corporate management was so impressed with his honesty that they declined his payment.

Painful memories resurfaced, accompanied by a deep-seated conviction about my need to make recompense for my old shoplifting transgression. The Lord began to speak to my heart. *My child, you know what you need to do. I will be with you, supporting, encouraging, and strengthening you. Yes, admitting your guilt will be difficult. It will require humility—for a prideful heart is incapable of admitting to failure and wrongdoing. But, take heart! I will go before you to prepare the way.*

God's words comforted and fortified me. What would have been impossible to accomplish in my own feeble strength, I knew I could do with the Lord's help. Resolving to be obedient, I prayed, "Okay, Lord. I'll do it. I trust You to keep Your promises. It's going to be scary and humiliating. But it's the only way I'll find peace."

Heart thumping in my chest, I entered the store several weeks later. I uttered a silent prayer for courage as I approached the checkout counter. "Hi. I'm here to make restitution for a shoplifting incident," I explained, filling in the details.

"I'm sorry, but you'll need to talk to the supervisor," the checker replied.

Oh, no. Now I'll have to humiliate myself all over again, I thought.

Finding the supervisor, I poured out my confession once more.

"Wow! I would not have had the nerve to admit my wrongdoing, as you just did," the young man marveled. "But our store cannot accept your payment. You'll need to contact the general manager. I'll jot down his address for you."

Exhaling a sigh of relief as I exited the store, I thought, *That wasn't nearly as difficult as I feared it would be. God surely did prepare the way. And mailing a check will be a piece of cake compared to this!*

About a month after I had sent off a check and an explanatory letter, I received a telephone call from the regional administrative assistant for the toy-store chain. "I'm so glad I was able to reach you," she began. "Your letter and check were forwarded to me by the general manager. I want to commend you for your honesty. Unfortunately, we are unable to accept your payment for accounting reasons. With your permission, however, we would be happy to donate the money to Toys for Tots."

"That's a great idea!" I responded.

Hanging up the phone, I thanked the Lord for the blessing He had just given me and for supporting me so I could do His will. Finally, I was able to forgive myself. I rejoiced that the heavy burden had been lifted and that I could be at peace.

Several months following this incident, I forwarded a copy of the confession letter to Dr. Sala. In the accompanying note, I thanked him for the testimony that had inspired me to make recompense.

Dr. Sala, in turn, sent me an autographed copy of his book, *Heroes*. In his letter, he wrote, "Sue, you are my hero for the day, and I am very proud of your integrity and what you did!"

Although I certainly don't feel like a hero, his message conveyed the sentiment I believe God desired to impart to me: *Well done, My child. I am so proud of you!*

FACING MYSELF

by Cecil Murphey

Whom the LORD loves He reproves,

even as a father, the son in whom he delights.

PROVERBS 3:12 NASB

The Bible was clear: If someone offended me, then I must forgive them. When Bud offended me, however, his words stung worse than any accusations that had ever been hurled at me. *How could he possibly think I could do those things?* I asked myself. In our hour-long argument, I tried to explain, but he wouldn't listen. The more I tried to clarify, the angrier he became.

That altercation took place less than four hours before my wife and I were scheduled to fly out of Kenya, East Africa. We had served there as missionaries for almost six years, and we were tired and eager to get back to the United States.

Earlier that day, Evelyn[19] , another missionary, asked me about a rumor of dissatisfaction from national leaders with Bud's leadership. I told her what several angry African leaders had said, and she promised to say nothing. Some wanted to complain to the civil authorities and have Bud forced out of the country. I had urged them not to take such a drastic measure. In fact, I pleaded with them to call for a meeting and lay out their complaints.

"He will not hear us. He never listens," one of them said.

"Regardless, you need to speak to him." I reminded them that the Bible said to go to the person first. They promised they would.

When Bud confronted me that evening, I learned that Evelyn had immediately gone to him. No matter what I said, Bud insisted that the Africans would not have told me those things if I hadn't been part of the problem.

"Why did they talk to you? If they had complaints, I'm the one they should have come to." Nothing I said calmed him down.

Bud insisted that we cancel our plans to return to the United States until we could get all the African leaders together two weeks later. I refused, and he denounced me in even stronger language.

We caught our flight; and by the time I reached the United States, I knew two things. I had to forgive Bud because that's what the Bible commands. I also wanted to forgive him because it was the right thing to do.

Like any good Christian, I asked God to enable me to forgive. "But he's wrong," I kept saying. I asked the Holy Spirit to search my heart and take away any wrongdoing on my part. Tears poured down my face, because I couldn't understand how Bud could treat me that way.

As I prayed, I remembered other times when he had hurt my feelings. For example, learning Swahili came easily for him, and he laughed at my pronunciation. Once he rebuked me in front of several missionaries because of the way I handled a situation, even though he hadn't been there and didn't know all the circumstances. I remembered other insults, short-tempered retorts, and harsh tones. Even though Bud was wrong, I had to forgive him if I wanted peace.

I don't know how long the intense hurt lasted, but it might have been as long as two weeks. Every time I thought of what he had said, I hurt. I prayed, "I forgive Bud; I forgive Bud. I don't care how wrong he is, I forgive him."

Eventually, Bud invaded my thoughts less often. After a while, I didn't think of him for weeks at a time. Whenever anything happened and his name came up, I could feel the pain, and I'd go through a time of protracted prayer to forgive him.

One day, missionary friends Ken and Helen Bennett visited us. When Bud's name came up, I said, "He was wrong in the way he treated me, but I've forgiven him."

"If you have forgiven Bud," Shirley asked, "why do you keep bringing up what he's done?"

Her words shocked me. I sputtered for a few seconds. "I-I guess you're right," I said.

After the Bennetts left, the old agony returned. Bud's angry words rang through my mind. I saw his blue eyes boring into mine, and I stared at his set jaw and down-turned lips. The pain was as intense as if the event had taken place only the day before.

For the next two days, I went about my work; but I still seethed inside. I finally decided I had to rid myself of my deep-seated pain. I prayed, but nothing happened. He's the one who was wrong. Why am I still suffering?

I asked God to forgive Bud. I went down the list of things he had done; and after each one, I asked God to forgive him and to release my pain. In desperation, I cried, "Oh, God, You know how badly he treated me and how evil he is and—"

I stopped. I grasped something new. For the first time, I began to think of the situation from Bud's point of view. I believed he sincerely loved God and attempted to serve Him faithfully. From his perspective, he had done the right thing.

Until then I had focused on the evil of his heart; but in that instant, I understood the man's sincerity. I also realized that when Evelyn's gossip had stirred him up, he was acting out of his own pain. He felt rejected and hurt. Why wouldn't he lash out at me?

This was the first time I thought about Bud's feelings. My actions had hurt him deeply. He had expected my loyalty and support. Instead, he felt I had turned against him by allowing the Africans to express their complaints to me instead of him. I felt Bud's pain. Tears fell from my eyes, but this time they came from a different source.

Then a second realization came to me. I heard myself asking: *Why did this hurt so badly?* Evelyn's going to Bud had caused the rift, and yet I hadn't felt any deep anger toward her. Why wasn't I as angry with her as I had been with Bud?

As I pondered that question, I realized something about myself. There had been truth in his accusations that I hadn't been able to hear. I hadn't plotted against Bud or taken any outward action against him, but I hadn't supported him, either. I had allowed the African leaders to speak against him—perhaps encouraged them by my silence or by my occasional agreement with their complaints.

Now I understood why the pain had been so intense. Bud's anger had triggered something evil in me. My inability to forgive had forced me to look at myself, and I didn't like what I saw. My pain was more about me than it was about him.

In effect, Bud was holding up a mirror for me to look at my careless words, minor hurts, and little resentments. I finally admitted to myself that I had been secretly glad because of the African leaders' discontent.

Rarely has that kind of insight cut so deeply into me. I know that when something evokes strong emotional reaction— good or bad—the reaction says more about us than it does about the other person or the event.

A wave of helplessness swept over me. How could I have been so stupid and so blind? I had been so self-righteous—seeing myself as good and continuing to rail, "But he's wrong."

The pain I had nursed and held on to had been my unwillingness to face myself and admit my failing. I knew God had forgiven me; now I struggled to forgive myself.

Finally, I wrote Bud a letter. "I don't care whose fault this was, and it's too late to sort it out. I'm writing to ask you to forgive me for the wrong I've done."

Not long after that, Bud wrote back. "I forgive you." Then—to my immense surprise—he asked me to forgive him.

The story ends nearly a year later. Shirley and I decided to fly to Denver to visit her brother. "Guess who's visiting our church this week?" Frank asked. "Your old friend Bud. He's coming to the pastor's house this afternoon, and I said I'd bring you along." Frank didn't know the story about our falling out.

I smiled and lapsed into silence, trying to figure out how I felt. I thought I had cleared away all the anger, but had I? Seeing Bud would be the test to find out if I had truly forgiven him and myself.

When Bud and I saw each other, we quickly walked toward each other with outstrectched arms; and we hugged each other. "Is everything okay between us?" I whispered.

"It sure is," he said and squeezed me again.

As I pulled away, I stared at his face. I detected no anger.

I became aware of three things. I had forgiven Bud even though he had been wrong. I had forgiven myself even though I had been wrong. Most of all, God had forgiven us both.

I was at peace.

The quality of mercy is not strain'd,

It droppeth as the gentle rain from heaven

Upon the place beneath: it is twice blest;

It blesseth him that gives, and him that takes.

WILLIAM SHAKESPEARE

RECEIVING FORGIVENESS

A man's pride brings him low,

but a man of lowly spirit gains honor.

PROVERBS 29:23

In order for us to be healthy and whole, we must both give and receive forgiveness. In receiving forgiveness from those we have hurt, the first thing we must do is often the most difficult—we must admit that we were wrong. Ouch!

Why is that so hard for us? The answer is pride. It requires us to admit that we aren't perfect. We are fallible. We make mistakes and do bad things. We feel vulnerable.

There is an exercise that many motivational speakers use to illustrate the importance that trust plays in relationships. You may have observed it, or perhaps you have even participated in the activity. It works like this. One person covers his eyes with a blindfold. The other individual is to stand directly behind him. On the count of three, the blindfolded person falls back into the arms of the second individual.

What if the "catcher" is someone with whom you've butted heads? What if the catcher takes advantage of the opportunity and lets you fall and hurt yourself? You don't have to actually participate in this exercise to get the point.

That's how it is when we ask someone to forgive us. Because we don't know what the individual's response will be, it is as if we walk into the situation blindfolded and place ourselves at the mercy of the one we've injured.

What if he uses the opportunity to get even? What if she ridicules me? What if I look like a fool? What if it gives him the upper hand? What if . . .

It's true—there is no guarantee that you will be well received or that there will be reconciliation, but it is a necessary step toward wholeness.

But let's assume that the person you hurt does want reconciliation. Their forgiveness is one of the most precious gifts you will ever receive. In effect, the individual is saying to you, "You and I both know what you did, but I forgive you. I ask God to forgive you, as well. I do not seek revenge. I refuse to think ill of you. If I experience negative emotions regarding the situation, I will take those feelings to God to receive His help in letting them go. I choose to do as God does and put your transgression out of my mind. I will not continually rehash it or lord it over you. I will not use it against you, nor will I gossip about the situation to others. I choose instead to bless you and only think positive thoughts about you. You are valuable to me."

When someone forgives you, something wonderful happens inside that person. He or she chooses to let go of the negative thoughts and feelings that have held them captive. It puts that individual in a position to receive peace and healing from God. It enables the person to move on.

But in order for you to experience the benefit of another's forgiveness, you must reach out and take what is being offered. Then you must let go of the situation the way your forgiver has. Only then will you find, as in the exercise with the blindfold, the relationship has entered a new level of deeper trust and mutual understanding. It's a blessing indeed.

WHO SPILLED THE BEANS?

Author Unknown

Jesus said, "Pray for those who hurt you."

MATTHEW 5:44 NCV

Many years ago, I accidentally spilled a sack of beans over the kitchen drain. I knew my husband was going to be angry at having to take the drain apart. But I didn't realize I was afraid of his anger until he came home and I heard myself blaming the incident on my eight-year-old daughter.

I truly didn't know I was going to lie until I did it. I can still remember the look of shock and disbelief on her face. She didn't call me a liar or burst into tears when her dad sent her to her room. I didn't have the courage to take it back immediately. It took me about ten minutes before I told my husband I had lied and that I was sorry for the lie and for the extra work I had made for him.

He is not abusive. I was just weak emotionally, and I guess I just didn't want to cope with the truth. But I was utterly ashamed of what I had done. When I went to find my daughter, she was sitting on her bed with her head down and her eyes closed. She was praying for me! She had forgiven me even before I had admitted the lie! I have never forgotten that experience. I tell her often that she is one of the best teachers I have ever had.[20]

Jesus told us that we are to become like little children if we are to enter the kingdom of heaven. Surely that includes being quick to forgive. But it also means being quick to receive the forgiveness of others, even when that forgiveness comes from a child.

"Yes, Daddy, I promise"

by Nancy C. Anderson

I acknowledged my sin to You, and my iniquity I did not hide;

I said, "I will confess my transgressions to the LORD";

And You forgave the guilt of my sin.

PSALM 32:5 NASB

The security guard grabbed my arm as his sharp words sliced through the air, "Come with me." He led me back inside the discount store and into the office. Then, he pointed to a lime-green chair and barked, "Sit down!"

I sat.

He glared at me and said, "You can give it to me—or I can take it—your choice. What'll it be?"

I wondered, *Should I lie? . . . Should I run? . . . Should I beg? . . . Yes, begging might work.* My head dropped into my hands as I pretended to cry, "Please—can't you just let me go? I can pay you. I have money in my pocket. I'm only fourteen years old. Please sir, I promise never to shoplift again." As I pulled the package of hair ribbons out of the waistband of my jeans, I could feel the sharp corner of the cardboard cutting into my stomach.

He grabbed the ribbons and said, "Save your tears; they

won't work on me. I'm sick of you bratty kids stealing, just for the thrill of it."

I sat up straight and pleaded, "You're not going to call my dad, are you?"

"I'm calling the police. They will call your father."

When the officers arrived, they exchanged muffled words with the guard and the office manager. I overheard one of the policemen say, "I know her father." I also heard the phrase, "Teach her a lesson." I began to cry—real tears.

The policemen escorted me to their black-and-white car and opened the back door. As we drove through the middle of our small town, I slouched down in the seat, hoping no one could see me as I looked out the window at the evening sky. Then, I saw the steeple of my family's church, and the guilt pierced me—swift and deep. *How could I have been so stupid? I thought. This is going to break my father's heart—and I've already broken God's. O Lord, please forgive me.*

We arrived at the station, and a round woman with a square face asked me questions until I ran out of answers. She pointed to the door of a large open cell and said, "Sit. Wait."

I walked in, and the sound of my footsteps bounced off the bars. The tears started again as I sat down on a hard bench and heard her dial the telephone. She said, "I have your daughter in a cell at the police station . . . No, she's not hurt . . . She was caught shoplifting. Can you come and get her? Okay . . . You're welcome, good-bye."

She yelled, "Hey kid, your father's on his way."

About one hundred years later, I heard Dad's voice say my name. The woman called me up to the desk—at three times the necessary volume. I kept my eyes on the floor as I walked toward them. I saw my dad's shoes but I didn't speak to him or look at his face; and thankfully, he didn't ask me to. He signed some papers, and my jailer told us, "You're free to go."

The night sky was dark and cold as we walked to the car in heavy silence. I got in and closed the door. He looked straight ahead as he drove out of the parking lot and whispered, in a sad, faraway voice, "My daughter is a thief."

The five-mile drive felt like it took forever. As we turned onto our driveway, I saw my mom's silhouette at the back door. My shame bit me with jagged teeth.

After we entered the house, Dad finally spoke to me, "Let's go into the living room." Mom and Dad sat together on the couch, and I sat alone, in the stiff wingback chair. He ran his fingers through his hair, looked into my eyes, and asked me, "Why?"

I told him about the first time I stole a tube of lipstick and how I felt equal amounts of thrill and guilt. Then the second time, when I took a teen magazine, the guilt faded as the thrill grew. Part of me wanted to stop the confession, but it gushed out like an open fire hydrant.

I told them about the third time, and the fourth, and the tenth.

I said, "Each time I stole, it got easier. Until now. I can see how wrong it was." Hot tears stung my face as I said, "I'm so sorry. Please forgive me—I promise never to do it again. Stealing was easy, but getting caught is hard."

Dad replied, "Yes, and it's going to get even harder." He asked Mom to hand me the notepad and pen that were sitting by the telephone. She walked over and patted my hand as she placed them in my lap. Dad continued, "Make a list of all the places you have stolen from, what you took, and how much it cost. This is your one chance for a full confession and our forgiveness. If you ever steal anything again, I will not defend you or bail you out. We will always love you, but this behavior is to stop, right here tonight. Do you understand?"

I looked at his face, which had suddenly aged, and said, "Yes, Daddy, I understand."

As I worked on my list of offenses, Mom said, "Make sure you haven't forgotten anything; this is your only chance."

Finally, I finished writing and said, "Here's the list." As I handed it to Dad, I asked, "What are you going to do with it?"

Dad looked at the paper and sighed. He patted the cushion, and I sat down between my parents. He said, "Sometimes forgiveness is just one step on the road to full restoration. The next step, in your case, is to pay restitution—to right the wrong. So tomorrow morning, we will go to all the places on your list, and you will speak to the managers. You will tell them that you have shoplifted from their stores. You will tell them exactly what you stole, apologize, and repay the store. I'll loan you the money, and you'll work all summer to pay me back."

With my heart slamming and my palms sweating, I nodded.

The next morning, I did exactly as he asked. It was impossibly hard, but I did it.

That summer, I repaid my father the money, but I will never be able to repay him for the valuable lesson he taught me about honesty, receiving forgiveness, and restoration. I never stole again.

MY FATHER'S GIFT

by Pamela Sonnenmoser

Thanks be unto God for his unspeakable gift.

2 CORINTHIANS 9:15 KJV

The car was filled with so many packages that I could hardly see out the back window. This would be the best Christmas ever. Sure, I had made some mistakes in the past few years, but this holiday at home would make up for it.

I married a few months before my twentieth birthday. My dad wouldn't even walk me down the aisle. He knew it was a mistake, and he told me so. I just didn't listen. Actually, I had never been very good at listening. There's a long list of things that happened in my life because I chose not to listen to my dad.

When I was eleven, he told me not to take the crutches stored in the garage. Then he told me to stay in the yard. As I swung between the crutches down the sidewalk to see my friends, I fell and broke my hip. I spent a year and a half recovering.

When I was seventeen, he told me not to leave campus for lunch. "The traffic is too heavy," he told me. My friend Bridgett spilled her chocolate shake all over the seat as a truck hit my driver's side door and turned my car into a horseshoe. We were okay except for the tiny shards of glass in our backs and arms from the breaking windows. I couldn't go off campus after that unless it was on foot.

On my nineteenth birthday, my dad told me to stay in school. He said that I should finish college before I tried to be an adult. Here I was, three years later. My marriage was over, and my life was a mess. It seemed I would never amount to anything. That's why this Christmas visit seemed so important. I saw it as my chance to change all that. I had to prove that I could make it on my own. I could hardly wait until my family opened the wonderful gifts I was bringing. I had worked over-time for the entire month of November to purchase the gifts I thought a good daughter should bring.

I sang Christmas carols with the radio from the glittering shores of San Diego to the extensive desert of Arizona's south-west corner. I loved the way radio stations dedicated all of Christmas Eve to the season.

As I pulled into my parents' familiar driveway, the sting from not-so-distant memories pricked my heart. I had never meant to hurt them. They just couldn't understand what I was going through. It wasn't that I didn't appreciate their help and advice, but it was my life. Singing at the club didn't make me a bad person. But Daddy didn't see it that way. The last time I was home, he refused to let me sing at the Sunday service. His words hurt me, but not half as much as the look of disappoint-ment that came with his lecture. I quit singing in the bar after that, but he still couldn't accept what my life had become.

This time would be different. I gathered as many gifts as I could in my arms and headed inside to put them under my mom's beautifully decorated tree. Three trips to the car and a steaming mug of mulled cider later, and I was ready to settle in for our traditional Christmas Eve.

For as long as I could remember, each member of my family opened all but one of our presents on Christmas Eve. This year was no exception. My dad began to pass out gifts to each person. I was so proud to note that so many of the gifts under the tree were from me. When everything had been passed out, one gift remained under the tree for each person to be opened in the morning. We had a wonderful time the rest of the evening. It felt as if the past had been wiped away. But I knew it was there, lurking around the next conversation or question. It had to come up. It always did.

Christmas morning, our stockings were hung on the artificial fireplace my mom had set up in the living room. My stocking had been a gift from a lady in the church that my dad pastored when I was a baby. The felt angels and golden rickrack were starting to peel at the edges, but there was something very reassuring about it being there. It was our tradition to open our stockings before breakfast.

Christmas breakfast was wonderful. Maple-sugar bacon filled the kitchen with its mouthwatering aroma. Dad made the best bacon ever. Mom cooked her famous omelet casserole while I prepared cranberry-walnut muffins. We met at the table where my brother served freshly squeezed orange juice from fruit he had picked from my uncle's trees at dawn. Breakfast was as lovely and wonderful as any I remembered.

With hearts as full as our stomachs, we made our way back to the Christmas tree in the living room. The final gifts were waiting. I could not imagine what was in the enormous box behind the tree. The tag had my name. I laughed as I opened it, realizing that it was my dad's favorite trick—a box, in a box, in a box, in a box. Each one wrapped with different paper. Finally, I got to the center. A beautiful silver box was tied shut with a simple gold thread. Scrolled into the lid was the word *kafar*, the Hebrew word for forgiveness. I opened the box. Tucked inside was a simple note.

"Pamela, I want you to know how much I love you. There is nothing you could ever do that could remove you from my heart. You are forgiven. The slate is clean. Love, Dad."

My tears ran freely as I wrapped my arms around my daddy's neck. The smell of Old Spice took me back to Christmas past when I would sit on his lap and open my Christmas morning gift. In those days, I never doubted his love. I never even thought about trying to buy the affection of my family with fancy gifts. I just knew they loved me.

I thought of my relationship with God. It had suffered in the past few years, as well. My dad's words echoed through my spirit as if my heavenly Father were saying the same thing. *There is nothing you can do that could remove you from My heart. Turn away from everything else and come back to Me. The slate can be made clean.*

That morning my dad and I spent time in prayer as I gave myself back to God. My tears ran freely as I wrapped my heart around the promises in His Word. The smell of spices from the kitchen took me back to the Christmas past when God sent a baby to bring the perfect gift of forgiveness into a world lost in sin. *How could I have ever doubted His love?* I wondered.

We said farewell to my dad a couple of years ago. Standing at his graveside, I held in my heart the greatest gift he ever gave me. As my mom, my brother, and I walked arm in arm through the warm April afternoon, I knew that Daddy was celebrating Christmas—the greatest gift he would ever receive.

THE FRAGRANCE OF VIOLETS

by Lois Williams

So overflowing is his kindness toward us that he

took away all our sins through the blood of his Son,

by whom we are saved; and he has showered down upon us

the richness of his grace.

EPHESIANS 1:7-8 TLB

I hurt my friend. I tried to steal her boyfriend. It was a long time ago, but I will never forget what I did and the lesson I learned from her.

We were seniors in high school. Traditionally, as graduation approached, the senior class chartered a bus and took a trip. Ours was a small-town school, and we decided it would be exciting to visit the big city. We pulled out of town at midnight, following the last performance of our class play. Our goal, after a six-hour drive, was Denver, the closest place to find bright lights and excitement.

We were all in high spirits and heady with the thrill of being on our own, except, of course, for our class advisors sitting in the front of the bus. Someone began a silly kissing game; and soon, we were changing seats and "telling secrets," our euphemism for kissing each other. I am not proud of my behavior that night, as I look back upon it. But I was desperate to be accepted and anxious to be popular; I wanted to show everyone that even the preacher's daughter could be just like the rest of them. I was having a marvelous time in the darkness of the bus, feeling a part of the crowd. It seemed harmless enough—until we got home.

In school the following Monday, my friend called me aside and told me how much I had hurt her by monopolizing the boy she really liked. I knew she liked him, and I had been free with my kisses, anyway. She said, "I was so angry with you that it spoiled my whole trip."

Her words made me feel small and cheap. I prayed that the floor would open and swallow me whole. I wanted to defend myself, but I knew what I'd done was wrong. I stammered, "I'm so sorry." And she said something I will never, ever forget: "I forgive you. I think I understand why you did it. We were all acting crazy. But you are my friend, and I had to tell you how disappointed I was in you. I care about you, though, and I forgive you. We can still be friends."

Mark Twain said that forgiveness is the fragrance a violet sheds upon the heel that crushes it. I believe it is an aroma of love that clears the air. It must be accepted as well as offered, however, for healing to be effective for both parties.

I have learned that in accepting forgiveness, we must respect the integrity of the person giving it. My friend showed me her character that morning—willing to confront, to share her pain honestly, and to give me an opportunity to help the healing process. She took the risk to restore a relationship that was valuable to both of us and added the sweet offer of forgiveness. My responsibility in the restoration of the bond between us was to accept that offer, to look her in the eye, and let the grace of her generosity wash over me.

Yes, it was a long time ago. But every time I hurt someone or am hurt by another person, I remember that day and the stunning perception of what it means to be forgiven. Looking back on that event helps me understand just what it means to accept the forgiveness that God offers. When God convicts us of wrongdoing, He always stands ready to forgive. Sometimes I feel unworthy of His forgiveness. I protest, unwilling to grab and hold on to His grace. But then I remember my friend and how good it felt knowing that she forgave me for the way I had wronged her. Our relationship was restored.

God paid a high price to redeem me. I must accept His offer of pardon because I know and respect the purity of His character—and His willingness to forgive. In the Old Testament, the people confessed their sin against the Lord. Part of their prayer contains these words: "But You are God, ready to pardon, gracious and merciful, slow to anger, abundant in kindness" (Nehemiah 9:17 NRSV).

Ready to pardon—longing for restoration—that is God's character. But I must accept His pardon. Sometimes I find it difficult to accept God's forgiveness without defending myself. I'm learning, though. And every time I reach out to clasp the hand of my God in repentance, I catch a whiff of the fragrance of violets.

VICTORY THROUGH SURRENDER

by Nancy C. Anderson

We capture every thought and make it give up and obey Christ.

2 CORINTHIANS 10:5 NCV

Dad boldly asked my husband and me, "What's your plan?"

Ron leaned forward, "Plan? Plan for what?"

"You two are going to have to figure out why your marriage fell apart . . . how to fix it . . . how to make sure it doesn't happen again."

Ron replied, "Well . . . I don't know if we need to do all that. I don't even want to talk about what she did. It's too painful. Nancy's back home now—we'll just move on from here."

Dad continued, "I wish it were that simple. But it's not. Your marriage was fractured. If you rebuild a house on a cracked foundation, then it might be all right for a while; but when the storms come, that fracture will divide your house. Ron, if you don't repair the foundation of your marriage, then it won't survive. You can't just ignore the fact that your wife had an affair. The memory of Nancy's betrayal and the guilt she will carry will be unbearable for both of you. I don't think you'll be able to move on until you, Ron, make one of the most important decisions you'll ever make."

"What decision is that?"

"Has Nancy told you she's sorry for what she's done?"

"Yes, she's apologized several times."

"Did she ask you to forgive her?"

"Not in those exact words."

Dad turned to me and continued, "Nancy, when you tell someone you're sorry, it's very different from asking for their forgiveness. Your 'sorry-ness' is your decision. But when you ask someone to forgive you—that's their decision. It's difficult because it gives all the power to the other person."

"That's a scary thought," I said without meaning to say it aloud.

Then he spoke to Ron, who looked confused and apprehensive. "Ron, when you forgive someone, you make a choice to banish the offense from your mind and your heart. Jesus said that after He forgives us, our sins are as far away as the East is from the West. In other words, they are pardoned. Not because we're not guilty, but because we are. Our pardon is undeserved—it's a gift to us from God. If you decide to pardon Nancy, you can never use her sin against her, and God will give you the strength to start a new life together. But if you choose not to forgive—if you want to hold on to the pain, or punish her and keep her wound open—if you choose that, I don't think you'll stay married."

My voice trembled as I asked my dad, "I want to ask Ron to forgive me, but what do I say?"

"Tell him what you want to be forgiven for and then simply ask him. Then Ron will decide whether or not to forgive. You ask; he answers. It's the simplest thing you two will ever do—and the hardest."

What if I ask Ron for mercy and he denies me?
In my husband's expression, I saw the wide-eyed face of a frightened twelve-year-old boy. I spoke quickly so that I wouldn't lose the safety of the moment. "Ron, I've betrayed you mentally, spiritually, and physically. I've lied to you and deceived you. I have no defense or excuse. I've sinned against God and you. Can you—will you please forgive me?"

He leaned forward, never letting go of my eyes. The little boy was gone as my strong and confident husband said, "Nancy, we have both done and said terrible things to each other. Our marriage was a mess—and a lot of it was my fault. But I take a stand today to change all that. You have betrayed me, but I choose to forgive you."

We both began to cry, and our tears mixed with the river of divine love that flowed through the room. Our hearts were knit together as we began again—with a solid foundation.

However, my personal foundation was still unstable. My lies had been so tangled with truth that I wasn't sure which was which. Slowly, I began to untie the knots of my life. I was relieved to be done with deceit; but because the deceitful shadows, exaggerations, and half-truths had been my companions for months, the light of the whole truth seemed harsh. It felt like walking out into full sunlight after watching an afternoon matinee in a dark theater. It took some time for my heart to adjust.

I was full of self-doubt and couldn't believe how easily I had been swept away by my feelings. I began to understand: "Above all else, guard your heart, for it affects everything you do" (Proverbs 4:23 NLT). I had been unguarded. I didn't plunge into sin—I drifted in, like floating on an air mattress and falling asleep only to wake up a half mile from shore. I had to swim with all my strength to pull my heart back to shore.

Jesus' words to the woman who was caught in adultery gave me comfort and direction: "Neither do I condemn you; go and sin no more" (John 8:11 NKJV). Jesus' command was simple—but its execution was hard. I struggled.

Ron forgave me—miraculously. He let go of the pain and moved into freedom. I, however, got stuck in the sorrow of regret. Receiving and believing in my forgiveness was tedious and treacherous. One step forward; three steps back. The memories kept surprising and haunting me—they could be triggered by the scent of a stranger's cologne or the melody of a song. The shame of past pleasures followed me.

One day, several months after our reconciliation, I asked Ron, "Do you still think about it?"

"No. You have never given me cause to worry about it happening again. You always call when you're going to be late or have a change in your plans. You don't flirt with other men the way you used to. You really have changed, making it easy for me to trust you again."

If only I could trust myself.

It was a wearisome journey. Eventually, though, I came to see that I would have to surrender to the forgiveness in order to free myself from the prison of shame. God and my husband had already given me the keys, but I had refused to use them. Finally, one day, I did.

I found my victory through surrender as I prayed, "Lord, I give up. I cannot carry this anymore. I know that You have forgiven me and so has Ron; and today, I choose to receive that forgiveness. Now I ask You for the strength to forgive myself. I let go of the guilt, the shame, the sorrow, and I choose to walk toward Your light. You have set free, so I am free indeed." (See John 8:36.)

I refused to entertain the stray thoughts anymore. Instead, I replaced them with images of the new life that Ron and I were building. I also discovered that telling the story of our marital resurrection helped me heal. It gave a purpose to our pain.

In 2004, twenty-four years after my affair, I wrote a book about our journey, *Avoiding the Greener Grass Syndrome,* with the hope that our story of forgiveness and restoration will help other couples prevent or forgive infidelity.

Ron and I recently celebrated our twenty-sixth anniversary, and I am thrilled to report that we are deeply and tenderly in love—with each other!

ROAD TRIP TO FORGIVENESS

by Pamela Sonnenmoser

Confess your faults one to another,

and pray one for another, that ye may be healed.

JAMES 5:16 KJV

We loaded the car in silence, politely placing our bags in the trunk of the shiny red convertible. The pinkish-yellow light of dawn created a surreal look in the rose garden next to the driveway. We seemed to be in the opening scene of a movie, watching each other in mechanical animation.

As my mother pulled the car out of the drive and headed down the street, a glimmer of hope began to slice through the horizon with the sunrise. In moments we were heading west, the rising sun on our backs and the wind in our hair.

Growing up we had been so close. My mother was the star of my world. I knew that she would always love me. She was always there for me—the perfect room mother when I was in elementary school and the perfect confidante in junior high. But somehow by my first year of college, we had become strangers.

The sun was beginning to reflect off the desert floor. The sky, now purple, was eagerly awaiting the arrival of the morning in the west. Mom pulled the Oldsmobile to the sandy shoulder of Interstate 8.

Our relationship had become even worse over the past few years. It seemed like we just kept trying to be close, only to hurt each other again and again. After Daddy died, we tried even harder, but old hurts don't disappear easily.

When I asked her to drive up the coast of California with me, she was excited. But now, neither of us seemed to be looking forward to our week without interruptions. The rented red convertible that should have been a bonus was beginning to feel like a prison—and we had only been driving for two hours.

I thought back to when I was a little girl. My mom would make up songs when we went on long trips. I began to sing my favorite childhood car song. In moments we were both singing, "Every mile we drive, we drive with Jesus. He is always in our car. Over hills and driving through the desert, He will always be our guide. Every mile we drive, we drive with Jesus. Check the oil, and kick the tires. He's our map, He paves the way before us. In His love we shall arrive."

I thought about the trip during which we made up that song. We were going to a lake north of Santa Barbara. We loved to go camping. It was beautiful at the lake. So peaceful and quiet, it was truly a break from all the busyness in our lives. I was twelve, and my life was sweet, good, and safe.

At lunchtime I took the wheel. The song had lessened the tension in the car, and we had begun to enjoy our trip—but we were still avoiding all the topics of conversation that I wanted desperately to talk about. There were so many things that should be said and that should be forgiven. I wanted real peace in our relationship, not just sugarcoating. I knew that Mom wanted the same thing.

I wanted to tell her that I was sorry for all the things that I had put her through early in my adult life. I wanted her to know that I knew how much she had sacrificed to help me so that I wouldn't end up in the streets. And, I wanted to thank her for praying for me so faithfully. Those things were difficult to say. Even thinking about them brought tears to my eyes. I was thankful for the wind flowing through the open car, drying my face before she noticed.

I married young. The week we eloped, my parents had gone out of town. We turned my mother's beautifully decorated and always clean and tidy home into a wreck while they were away. Thinking about that as I drove the winding roads toward Malibu made me sick. I could imagine how she must have felt when she arrived home. As she walked in the door, she was greeted by a son-in-law and a kitten, neither of whom had lived there before. The smell of stale beer and rotting food had permeated her home. In our frenzy to try to clean up the mess we had made, nothing was done correctly. It took my mom two weeks to put her house back into order and two weeks after that to tell me she needed us to find another place to live right away.

The next three years were a roller-coaster ride of bad choices and heartache. My Marine husband was transferred to Camp Pendleton. My family didn't have to watch everything that happened; but for years, they felt the effects as they tried to help me out of all of my financially and emotionally damaging choices. They constantly tried to help me as my marriage crumbled into a sea of abuse and hatred. I was twenty-three, and my life seemed hopeless.

Mom must have seen my tears because she reached over

and brushed them off my face. That touch opened the flood-gates, and my silent tears became sobs. I pulled to the side of the road and sat there crying. When I looked up, I could see tears on Mom's cheeks, too. As the flood of emotion subsided, we smiled at one another. Not a condescending smile or a sympathetic smile, but a smile between friends that said, It's going to be okay. I understand that you are hurting, and I'm here for you.

By this time we were in Solvang, which had been our family's favorite weekend getaway during the years when everything was good. We found a little café and stopped for supper. As we enjoyed our Danish meal, we talked about so many things we had forgotten. And, I told my mother all of the things I needed to tell her. She listened so intently, almost like she was hearing about the things I had done for the first time.

Finally, she took my hand and said, "Sweetheart, I was not a perfect mother. I made mistakes, too. I love you, and I love the woman you have become. That is what grace is for. When we make mistakes, He picks us up and sets us on solid ground again. All we have to do is ask."

I was crying again, but she continued. "I forgave you for all of those things years ago. You just didn't take them off of your hook and put them on God's."

Then she said words that I hadn't expected. "I need you to forgive me, too. I know that there were times in your life that I let you down. I know that things didn't always seem fair, and sometimes I didn't handle my anger toward you the way I should have. I need you to forgive me, too."

Forgive you? Of course I forgive you. You're my mom. I assumed that she knew I had forgiven her. But she didn't. I needed to tell her. As I said those words that seemed so small, something wonderful happened. All the years of trying to figure out why we couldn't get along just melted away. A love for my mom filled my heart and the peace of Jesus that passes understanding covered our relationship.

As we got back in the convertible and continued our trek west, the sun was sinking into the Pacific Ocean with all of the pink and orange paint that it needed to create an elaborate watercolor. We reached the beach just as the bright orange orb was beginning to sizzle into the sea. Arm in arm, we stood watching the sunset as the daystar took all of our pain into the depths of the sea of forgetfulness and disappeared.

ENDNOTES

1. "Mansion Builder" words and music by Annie Herring. Copyright © 1978 by Latter Rain Music. All rights controlled and administered by The Sparrow Corporation, P.O. Box 2120, Chatsworth, CA 91311. All rights reserved. International Copyright Secured. Used by Permission.
2. Article found at Web site for First United Methodist Church of Canandaigua, http://www.canandaiguamethodist.org/Sermons/2001/2001-01-28.htm (accessed September 2004).
3. The Christian Broadcasting Network, Inc. © 2004.
4. Reprinted by permission from *Voice* magazine (Lake Forest, CA: Full Gospel Business Men's Fellowship International, December 1988).
5. Rolf Garborg, *The Family Blessing* (Lakeland, FL: White Stone Books, 2003) pp. 121-125. Reprinted by permission.
6. See www.HisPeace.org for additional information.
7. © Peacemaker® Ministries. Adapted by permission. www.HisPeace.org.
8. Karen Hardin, *Seasons of Love* (Lakeland, FL: White Stone Books, 2005). Excerpt reprinted by permission.
9. Adapted from http://www.inspirationalstories.com/6/608.html. (Accessed September 2004.)
10. Adapted from *Stolen Hours* by John Howard Prin, (St. Paul, MN: Syren Books, 2004 ISBN 0-929636-21-X). Excerpt adapted by permission.
11. Adapted from Janet Eckles, *Trials of Today, Treasure for Tomorrow*, (Xulon Press, 2004) Chapter 20. Used by permission.
12. Karen Hardin, *Seasons of Love* (Lakeland, FL: White Stone Books, 2005). Excerpt adapted by permission.
13. Adapted from Sydna Massé, *Pastor's Family*-December 1998/January 1999 (Ramah International, 1776 Hudson St., Englewood, FL 34223; (941) 473-2188. See www.ramahinternational.org for additional information.
14. James C. Dobson, *Straight Talk to Men and Their Wives* (Waco, TX: Word Books, 1980) p. 174.
15. Ibid., p. 178.
16. Gerhard Kittel, *Theological Dictionary of the New Testament*, Volume 1 (Grand Rapids, Michigan: Wm. B. Eerdmans, 1964) p. 509.
17. The freedom ministry at my church was based loosely on Neil Anderson's steps to freedom. For more information visit: www.ficm.org.
18. This list is based on one from Freedom in Christ ministry. Theirs can be downloaded at www.ficm.org./whoami.htm.
19. Not her real name.
20. Article found at http://www.forgiving.org/stories/read_detail.asp?uniqueID=7 (accessed September 2004). Reprinted by permission.

Additional copies of this and other
Honor Books products are available
from your local bookseller.

The following titles are also available from Honor Books:

Soul Sanctuary

Be Patient, God Isn't Finished with Me Yet!

Intimate Moments with God

If you have enjoyed this book,
or if it has had an impact on your life,
we would like to hear from you.

Please contact us at:

Honor Books, Dept. 201
4050 Lee Vance View
Colorado Springs, CO 80916
Or visit our Web site:
www.cookministries.com

HONOR **HB** BOOKS

Inspiration and Motivation for the Seasons of Life